Wise Parenting

❧ ♥ ❧

Wise Parenting

Guidelines from the Book of Proverbs

Paul and Catherine Wegner and Kimberlee Herman

DISCOVERY HOUSE

P U B L I S H E R S®

Feeding the Soul with the Word of God

Discovery House Publishers is affiliated with RBC Ministries,
Grand Rapids, Michigan.

Discovery House books are distributed to the trade exclusively by
Barbour Publishing, Inc., Uhrichsville, Ohio.

Requests for permission to quote from this book should be directed to: Permissions Department, Discovery House Publishers, P.O. Box 3566,
Grand Rapids, MI 49501.

Library of Congress Cataloging-in-Publication Data
Wegner, Paul D.
    Wise parenting : guidelines from the book of Proverbs / Paul and
Catherine Wegner and Kimberlee Herman.
        p.   cm.
    Includes bibliographical references.
    ISBN 978-1-57293-352-1
    1. Child rearing—Religious aspects—Christianity. 2. Child rearing—
Biblical teaching. 3. Descipline of children—Biblical teaching.
4. Parenting—Religious aspects—Christianity. 5. Parenting—Biblical
teaching. 6. Bible. O.T. Proverbs—Criticism, interpretation, etc.
I. Wegner, Catherine. II. Herman, Kimberlee. III.Title.
BV4529.W44 2009
248.8'45—dc22
                                                    2009042824

Printed in Canada

09 10 11 12 13 / 10 9 8 7 6 5 4 3 2 1

To our sons —
May they enjoy the pleasure and happiness
with their children that they have brought to our lives.
Love,
Paul and Cathy

To my darling daughter Madison —
The Lord has blessed and entrusted us with you,
a true gift of immense love. You have already opened
my eyes to a new level of understanding.

Thank you, Dave, for being my hero, my love,
and my companion. You are an incredible father.
Madison and I are so blessed to have you in our lives.
Love,
Kimberlee

Contents

*Children are a gift from the L*ORD*;*
they are a reward from him.
—PSALM 127:3

*Dear Lord, we lift up the parents who are reading this
book, parents who have turned to you for guidance in
raising the children you have blessed them with. We pray
that you will open their hearts and minds to follow the
divine wisdom you have laid out for us in the book of
Proverbs. In Christ we pray. Amen.*

Acknowledgments

Throughout this book our friend Kimberlee Herman, who is a clinical social worker, shares relevant stories from her experiences working with children and families across all socio-economic backgrounds and faiths. These clinical examples help demonstrate how some families are already using the parental wisdom in Proverbs. She also shares what it looks like when parents don't follow the guidelines laid out in Proverbs.

To protect the identity of the families Kimberlee has worked with and maintain confidentiality, she has changed the names of individuals and sometimes the circumstances in which certain events occurred.

1

Help!

While I was sitting at the food court in a shopping mall, two families caught my eye. Each family had two children, a boy and a girl, but there the similarity ended.

The first family had a clean-cut, energetic boy about five years old with Buzz Lightyear emblazoned on his shirt, and a calm, well-mannered girl about twelve years old with hints of makeup on her face and well-styled blonde hair. What caught my attention was that these kids were so well-behaved. They came when they were called and stopped picking on each other when told to do so. They even appeared to enjoy being around their parents.

The second family had a boy about ten years old, dressed in a Led Zeppelin T-shirt and blue jeans, and a girl about seven years old wearing blue short-shorts. What I noticed about these kids was that they were constantly whining and complaining, and it was obvious they didn't want to be shopping, at least with their parents. They had kicked into "how to get out of the mall the fastest way possible" mode.

What was even more disturbing was that their parents did just about everything to coax these two into cooperating. First, they offered ice cream cones, then a trip to the toy store, and finally, a ride on the merry-go-round. Each of these offers seemed to placate the children for about five minutes and then they were back to bickering, pouting, and aggravating each other. The parents had clearly lost control and were like puppets in the hands of these children. If there was a class on how to make your parents miserable in the local mall (and it seems like it must be mandatory for a lot of young children), then these two could have taught it.

I wondered how it was possible for a child to come out of the womb so beautiful and innocent and yet within six or seven short years become Darth Vader's clone. We have all been there—and for some of us it happens so often that we wonder if there is any way our incorrigible kids will ever transform into mature, conscientious adults.

So why were the children in the first family so well-behaved? How did those parents do it? Is there a secret to raising well-disciplined kids? Are there any disciplinary guidelines for parents to follow?

> Children are getting less moral and ethical direction from their parents at a time when they need and want it more. Left in a "belief" vacuum, they may determine from advertising and the media that white teeth and material possessions will make them happy and that life crises can be resolved in a half-hour format.

Help from Proverbs
We have written this book to provide answers to these questions, as well as hope for those parents who may be tempted to give up. In doing so, we will take you to the book of Proverbs in the Old Testament where God has provided us with many guidelines on how to discipline. In fact, the main purpose for the book of Proverbs is to teach the next generation how to live wisely, as the introduction points out:

The purpose of these proverbs is to teach people wisdom and discipline, and to help them understand wise sayings. Through these proverbs, people will receive instruction in discipline, good conduct, and doing what is right, just, and fair. These proverbs will make the simpleminded clever. They will give knowledge and purpose to young people.

Let those who are wise listen to these proverbs and become even wiser. And let those who understand receive guidance by exploring the depth of meaning in these proverbs, parables, wise sayings, and riddles (Proverbs 1:2–6).

It's easy to miss the important subtleties of Proverbs, however, so we'd like to walk you through what this book says about discipline. For example, people often take one or two verses from Proverbs to develop a whole system of discipline for their children:

- If you refuse to discipline your children, it proves you don't love them; if you love your children, you will be prompt to discipline them (13:24).
- Don't fail to correct your children. They won't die if you spank them. Physical discipline may well save them from death (23:13–14).

Some assume that these two verses provide a complete rationale for discipline and don't bother to look any further. As a result, this misunderstanding of Proverbs is sometimes used to justify the abuse of children—something the Bible never intended.

In April 2001, Rev. Arthur Allen, Jr., a man who had for thirty-five years been the pastor of a small church called The House of Prayer in Atlanta, was charged with cruelty to children. Two children in his congregation who had been unruly in school were whipped, leaving a seven-year-old with welts and bruises and a ten-year-old with open wounds on his belly and side. This same pastor had been jailed for thirty days in 1993 after ordering a sixteen-year-old girl whipped with belts, a beating that he admitted may have lasted for almost half an hour. Allen justified his actions based upon Proverbs 23:13, "Although you strike him with the rod, he will not die" (NASB).

But is this really what the book of Proverbs is proposing? The answer is emphatically "No!"

> More than 2.5 million cases of child abuse and neglect are reported each year. Of these, 35 of 100 involve physical abuse, 15 of 100 involve sexual abuse, and 50 of 100 involve neglect. Studies show that 1 in 4 girls and 1 in 8 boys will be sexually abused before they are 18 years old. About 1 in 20 children are physically abused each year.

What Does Proverbs Really Teach?

The book of Proverbs, when taken as a whole, encourages parents to use multiple levels of discipline, ranging from pointing out improper behavior to the use of corporal punishment. These levels fall into three main categories:

Step One: Teaching the Guidelines
Step Two: Reiterating the Guidelines
Step Three: Enforcing the Guidelines

Children aren't born knowing everything they will need to know to become mature, responsible human beings. Parents need to teach them these principles one by one. *Teaching these guidelines is Step One.*

Proverbs offers a variety of levels of discipline to help children learn these guidelines. Keep in mind that it is normal for children to test these guidelines to be sure their parents really believe they are important. So *reiterating the guidelines is Step Two.*

To help parents underscore the importance of these guidelines, in Step Two they may need to add some form of gentle discipline (e.g., time outs, or withholding a favorite toy, activity, or privilege) to emphasize that the guidelines are for the child's good and need to be followed.

> Bug us a little. Be strict and consistent in dishing out discipline. Show us who's boss. It gives us a feeling of security to know we've got some strong supports under us. (Part of the "Discipline Code for Parents" that was created by youth confined in a Pennsylvania correctional institution.)

If a child continues to push the boundaries, *Step Three is enforcing the guidelines.* At this point, after the other levels of discipline have failed to curb improper behavior, non-abusive corporal punishment (a spanking) may be necessary.

These progressive levels of discipline have been used successfully for generations to curb misbehavior. But did you know that this structure of discipline comes directly from the book of Proverbs? And did you also know that God uses the same type of discipline with us?

God's Use of Discipline

Often our modern generation sees discipline or correction as a bad thing. But the Bible says that God, as our heavenly Father, corrects us because He loves us. Proverbs 3:12 states it this way:

> The Lord corrects those he loves, just as a father corrects a child in whom he delights.

Our relationship with our heavenly Father is based upon love and grace, not performance. God loves us no matter how we act or what we do. Nothing will change His love for His children, even though He corrects us for our own good.

Our children also need to know that they are unconditionally loved by us. We discipline them because we love them, just as our heavenly Father disciplines us because He loves us.

Learning to Discipline Properly

Our own backgrounds and experiences can affect how we discipline and how we view discipline. For example, our good friend Norm had a father who was a mean-spirited man; thus, at an early age Norm began to equate discipline and fear.

Those who have had negative childhood experiences often want to do better with their own children. Those who have had a positive childhood want to emulate that with their children. But no matter how good or bad the examples were in your own family, there is always room for improvement.

Proper discipline must be done in love and safety or it will never have its intended result. We must build quality relationships with our children so that they know our hearts; otherwise, discipline will always be seen as punishment and not as refining or improving their character.

We must remember, however, that it is difficult to hold a proper balance between grace and truth. To help us, Scripture lays out the best guidelines, and we can learn and improve our parenting skills by examining them. And Jesus himself is the perfect blend between grace and truth:

> The Word became flesh, and dwelt among us, and we saw His glory, glory as of the only begotten from the Father, full of grace and truth (John 1:14 NASB).

The Law was given through Moses; grace and truth were realized through Jesus Christ (John 1:17 NASB).

In biblical terms, *grace* is unmerited favor. *Grace* is receiving something that we do not deserve. There are times when a parent needs to show grace when disciplining a child. For example, when a teenager has been caught speeding and been ticketed by the police, and then shows proper remorse and understanding of the seriousness of the offense, he or she has probably been punished enough. This would be an appropriate time to show a little grace and forgiveness.

Truth is laying out clearly what behavior is inappropriate and what punishment will be forthcoming for such behavior. Often children will push the boundaries of inappropriate behavior to make sure those boundaries are secure and that the parent is indeed going to enforce them.

There are times when either of these responses—grace or truth—is the correct response. If we always tend toward truth, however, our children may see us as inflexible guardians of the rules. And if we always tend toward grace, then it will be difficult for us to enforce the boundaries when a child has crossed them.

We place boundaries in our children's lives for their own good. No matter how difficult they may sometimes be to enforce, those boundaries help provide a safety net for our children.

During initial construction on the Golden Gate Bridge, no safety devices were used and 23 men fell to their deaths. For the final part of the project, however, a large net was used as a safety precaution. At least 10 men fell into it and were saved from certain death. Even more interesting, however, is the fact that 25% more work was accomplished after the net was installed. Why? Because the men had the assurance of their safety, and they were free to wholeheartedly serve the project.

There is a fine balance between grace and truth, and a good relationship with our children is the only way to monitor how we are doing with this balance. Since our personality can affect how we discipline, this is an area where husbands and wives can complement each other's strengths and weaknesses to maintain a proper balance.

We realize that in our modern society there are many single-parent families, and thus these parents are on their own in determining a proper balance between grace and truth. For parents in this situation, we recommend finding a friend with whom you can discuss parenting decisions. It will help both of you to make sure you maintain a proper balance of grace and truth with your children.

Parenting Styles

As you think about your own personality and how that might affect your parenting, consider these four types of parenting styles:

Permissive parents—tend to be too lenient, do not set good boundaries, are not demanding, and do not expect their children to act their age. They also avoid confrontation. Their children often grow up to be reckless, bossy, and aggressive adults who tend to have low self-control and lack achievement.

Authoritarian parents—tend to be demanding, but not responsive to their children. They focus on obedience and orders to be followed, with little or no flexibility. Their rules are clear and rigid and they use punishment to control behavior. Their children tend to become unhappy, anxious, resentful, stressed, and unfriendly adults.

Uninvolved parents—don't respond and don't demand. They are unavailable to their children and may even reject their children. Their children tend to look to other people as role models (often inappropriate people, since no one has helped them learn how to choose good role models); they also have low self-esteem and lack confidence.

Authoritative parents—have a good balance between responsiveness and demands. They set clear standards for their children, but they are also supportive and encouraging. They are not punitive, but have clear guidelines that the children are expected to follow. They control their children's behavior by explaining rules with discussion, not demands. When the boundaries or guidelines are crossed, there is some form of discipline administered that has already been clearly specified. They listen to their children, even when they do not agree with them. Their children tend to develop into friendly, cheerful, cooperative adults.

It is apparent that this last type of parenting style, the authoritative parent, is the best—a balance between nurturing and guidelines. This parenting style will raise the most well-adjusted and emotionally healthy children. It is interesting that this is the parenting style described in Proverbs. However, being a good parent is a process, and there will be times that we do a great job and other times that we will fail miserably. It will be times like the latter that draw us back to our heavenly Father to ask Him for help and guidance in raising our children.

So with a prayer that God will make us better parents, let's get started on our journey to understanding wise parenting and hopefully becoming wise parents.

STUDY QUESTIONS

To get the most out of this book, think about the following questions before moving on to the next chapter.

1. What is your parenting style: permissive, authoritarian, uninvolved, or authoritative?

2. Do you feel your parenting style is effective? Is it helping you to have a close relationship with your children?

3. What is your family background and how has it affected your parenting? Are there good things that you want to emulate? Are there specific things that you would like to do better?

4. What is your spouse's family background and how has it affected your parenting? Are there good things that you want to emulate? Are there specific things that you would like to do better?

5. Which do you lean toward, grace or truth?

   Me:

   My Spouse:

6. How could your spouse's parenting style complement yours and vice versa?

   Me:

   My Spouse:

7. If you are a single parent, is there a family you know that appears to have well-adjusted children? If so, could you talk over some of their parenting tips with them? Ask them if they would mind a phone call at times when you are uncertain what to do or when you are having a problem.

TIME TO PRACTICE

Think about the best way to handle the following situations:

Mandy is five years old and she regularly takes toys from other children at pre-school or when they come over to play at her house. Generally it turns into a shouting match and sometimes even a hitting match. What should her mother do?

A fifteen-year-old boy tells his best friend he wants to have sex with his new girlfriend. The fifteen-year-old boy's father overhears this. What should the father do?

2

Where It All Begins – Laying the Foundation

Teach your children to choose the right path, and when they are older, they will remain upon it.

—PROVERBS 22:6

One of the greatest joys of a parent is to see a son or a daughter grow into a mature, loving adult. It is a proud moment when someone comments that your son has turned into a real gentleman or your daughter has become a sweet and kind young lady. At times like that even the most insecure parents actually believe that they might have done something right.

The ultimate goal of child-rearing is to take that newborn bundle of joy and gradually, over the next two decades, mold him or her into a mature, responsible, loving adult. It is a 24/7 job that will change the parent as much as the child. There will be times of delight, as well as times of worry and frustration. Progress will often be offset by setbacks and failures. When your child reaches about age thirteen, you may think you'll have to start over again from scratch. But little by little manners and small acts of kindness will appear. Before long your children are not fighting as much with their brothers and sisters, and finally hope dawns that this child may become a positive member of society.

The hope of every parent is to have children who are responsible, concerned members of society. Discipline is, of course, part of this effort. Research has repeatedly shown that, despite the importance of the peer group, parents usually have much more influence than they realize. Disciplining children takes a great deal of effort but the main idea is that children and parents can change.

What Is the Point of Discipline?

Some parents believe that goodness and morals are inherent within children—all they need to do is to foster those good traits and allow them to develop. Reasoning and encouragement are expected to draw out appropriate behavior in their children. Yet the Scriptures tell us that every one of us is born with a sinful nature—in other words, our children are prone to misbehave. They come by it naturally. And it is our responsibility as parents to help curb their misbehavior and foster good behavior.

One winter I was playing outside with my oldest son, who was then five. The snow was perfect for packing, and we had a wonderful time making snow angels, throwing snowballs, and building a snow fort. When my wife called out to say dinner was ready, my son did not want to stop playing. He was having too much fun, even though the sun was going down and we were both tired and cold. No amount of coaxing seemed to change his mind. Finally I said, "Son, we have to go in now. It's getting cold and Mom has food waiting for us."

"No!" he blurted out defiantly. "That's the way I want it and that's the way it's gonna be."

We laugh about it now, but it's a good picture of the strong will we all start out with. Unless that will is curbed, we'll continue to do whatever pleases us and suffer the consequences.

Parents have the primary role and responsibility to nurture their young children (whose whole world revolves totally around themselves) and raise them into caring, mature adults. It is one of the most difficult tasks we have in this world, but also one of the most important. The social and spiritual health of the next generation depends upon how well we do our job.

Proverbs 29:15 says, "To discipline and reprimand a child produces wisdom, but a mother is disgraced by an undisciplined child." The heart of discipline is to teach wisdom. This is why the book of Proverbs is perfect for helping us learn to discipline, because the goal of Proverbs is to teach wisdom in every area of life, and it does so in a practical manner.

Discipline is a great gift to your children. You do them no favors by failing to teach them obedience when they are young, helping them to mature and prepare for all the responsibilities of adulthood. Are you willing to step up and at times make tough decisions so that you can give your children the gift of discipline? If not, you are setting them up for failure in the future.

Proverbs Has the Answer

The book of Proverbs provides a plan that encourages parents to use multiple levels of discipline. In fact, the Hebrew word *mûsar,* often translated as "discipline" in the Old Testament, has a wide range of meanings that suggest various levels of discipline. At one end of the spectrum there is teaching or instruction (Proverbs 1:2, 3, 7; 4:13); this progresses to exhortation or warning (Proverbs 6:23) and climaxes with punishment or chastening (Proverbs 3:11; 13:24; 22:15; 23:13).

Webster's New Collegiate Dictionary defines discipline as "training that corrects, molds, or perfects the mental faculties or moral character of a person." Applying this to the discipline of children implies an ongoing responsibility of parenthood, from infancy to at least late teens. But this does not mean that the same disciplinary techniques should be used throughout this process or that spanking should be the primary disciplinary technique. The wise parent understands the principle of using the least amount of discipline to curb improper behavior.

KIMBERLEE SAYS:

Jamie, a young vibrant mother of two, came into my office with her children. When they were leaving, her son Logan, age three, decided he was going to take one of my toy cars home with him. Jamie calmly asked him to leave it, and he told her "No, I want it." Jamie then quietly bent down, looked him in the eye, gently took his hands (and the toy) into hers and asked him to tell her about the toy. He told her that he liked it because it was blue and he did not have a blue one at home. She agreed with him and told him it sounded like it was important that he have a blue car at home. He nodded yes. She explained that this toy lived in the office and wanted to stay there, but that next time he got a toy, he could pick a nice blue one for his room. This worked!

When I reflected on this later, I realized that Jamie understood that for some reason the toy was important to Logan, and she validated this to him. She also made sure he understood that things have "homes" and you can't just take them. Lastly, she gave him hope that he would get his own blue car in the future. What a wise mother!

Each child is different, and wise parents learn what types of discipline will be most effective for an individual child. I have two boys, and when one of them was about eighteen months old, we told him to be very careful near the stove because sometimes it was hot and could burn him. He learned this lesson so well that whenever he walked by the stove he would point to it and say "hot, hot, hot" whether it was on or not. My other son was just the opposite. When we told him that the stove might be hot, the first thing he wanted to do was touch it. So for one son I could caution him with words and he modified his behavior appropriately. For the other son, I had to hold his hands so that he wouldn't reach out and touch the stove before cautioning him about it—he needed something a little more than words to curb his behavior.

It's not always easy to know how to discipline in each situation, but wise parents will have multiple levels of discipline at their command and be prepared to use them with increasing severity until inappropriate behavior is curbed. Children are smart and learn quickly. But they also remember if they got away with a certain behavior in the past. They expect parents to be consistent or have a good reason why they're not. Children also expect a certain amount of justice, and they need to feel they're being treated fairly and consistently.

When I was about ten years old, I placed something on the Bible. My father slapped me and said, "Don't ever place anything on top of the Bible." I remember thinking to myself, *He could have just said, "Don't place anything on the Bible" and I would have listened.* For my father to slap me when I didn't know his expectation was more severe than necessary.

Multiple Levels of Discipline

The multiple levels of discipline described in the book of Proverbs have some degree of overlap, but they begin with gentle instruction. In reality, good parents already do a certain amount of instructing and disciplining even without knowing it. When we purchase a certain type of car or choose to attend church, we are instructing our children about what we feel is important. When a mother says, "No, Stephanie! You can't go out of the house in that short skirt," she is disciplining her child by helping her know the difference between what is and what is not appropriate.

> Discipline properly involves a multifactorial approach that makes use of models, attitudes, rewards, and punishments to teach and reinforce socially acceptable behavior. Through discipline, children become able to achieve self-control, self-direction, and a sense of caring.

Parenting is a skill that takes effort, training, and patience. And if we make mistakes—and we will—God can oversee and redeem the process. When we as parents make a mistake or use poor judgment, we need to admit it and ask for God's help and our children's forgiveness. We don't have to do this job alone—God is always active in the process.

Above all, the most important thing that we can model to our children is that we love them no matter what they do. Our love does not depend upon their obedience—we will love them anyway.

Molding the will is a difficult job, but if we begin when our children are young, using lower levels of discipline, hopefully we will seldom have to use anything more severe.

Parenting is a skill that takes as much effort, training, and patience as any other type of artistic work. Even if we make mistakes, and we will, God can oversee the process if we will allow Him.

In 1502, a large block of marble was given to the church of Santa Maria in Florence, Italy. The church immediately hired an artist to sculpt this enormous piece of rock. Soon after commencing this monumental task the man drilled a hole through the bottom, destroying the magnificent piece of marble. The church leaders were greatly perplexed and, not knowing what else to do, decided merely to drape a huge sheet over it and hide it from view. When a man named Michelangelo heard of this large stone and how it had been destroyed, more out of curiosity than anything else he came to see it. After examining it closely, he believed that the enormous stone could still be salvaged and set to work. In time, that which was once thought to be a lost cause became one of the greatest statues of David ever created.

Our work is cut out for us—God has loaned us our children to shape into masterpieces. Even if they have been damaged or feel like they are useless, God can still remold and shape them into usable vessels. When we as parents make a mistake or use poor judgment, we need to admit it and ask for our children's forgiveness. But God expects us to do our very best with what we have been given. No one said it would be easy, and we don't have to do this job alone—God is active in the process. Also, the most important thing that we can model to our children is that we love them no matter what they do. Our love should not depend upon their obedience—we will love them anyway.

> Statistics indicate that the prevalence of parental disen-
> gagement is 25-30 percent, and one-quarter of American
> adolescents are not sure that their parents love them.

The following chart shows the various levels of discipline outlined in the book of Proverbs. We've divided them into three categories: 1) teaching the guidelines; 2) reiterating the guidelines; and 3) enforcing the guidelines—with principles under each category.

PRINCIPLES OF DISCIPLINE	BIBLICAL REFERENCES
Level 1: Teaching the Guidelines	
Principle 1: Teach Appropriate Behavior	Proverbs 1:8-9; 2:1-22; 3:1-35; 4:1-13; 6:20-26; 7:1-5; 8:1-36; 23:24-25
Principle 2: Inform of Improper Behavior	Proverbs 1:10-19; 4:14-27; 6:1-19; 7:6-21; 9:13-18; 22:24-25; 23:26-28
Principle 3: Explain the Negative Consequences of Disobedience	Proverbs 1:10-33; 5:1-23; 6:26-35; 7:22-27; 9:17-18; 10:1; 13:18; 14:14; 16:18, 26; 17:20; 18:13; 23:10-12; 24:17-20
Level 2: Reiterating the Guidelines	
Principle: Give Appropriate Warnings	Proverbs 1:7, 15, 19, 22, 28, 31-33; 2:11-19, 22; 3:7, 11; 4:2, 5-6, 14-19, 23-27; 5:3-16, 21-23; 6:1-5, 9-15, 25-35; 7:24-27; 8:33-36; 9:13-18; 10:1-24:34; 26:17-29:27; 31:2-9
Level 3: Enforcing the Guidelines	
Principle 1: A Reprimand with Non-Corporal Punishment	Proverbs 1:8; 3:12; 4:1-2, 10-27; 5:1-2; 6:1-5, 20-35; 7:1-5, 24-27; 23:22-23;24:24-25; 25:12; 27:5-6; 28:23
Principle 2: A Reprimand with Non-Abusive Corporal Punishment	Proverbs 13:24; 19:18; 23:13-14; 29:15
BEYOND A PARENT'S RESPONSIBILITY	
Level 4: Government's Role in Discipline *WARNING!*	
Principle: Continued Disobedience May Bring Severe Punishment	Proverbs 10:31; 20:30
[You will notice that Level 4 discipline falls outside the parent's responsibility, and we will look at this level later in the book. Even in Israel certain forms of punishment were not administered by parents (see Deuteronomy 21:18–21).]	

INCREASING SEVERITY

To get a clearer understanding of these various levels of discipline, let's liken the process of parenting to teaching someone how to drive. When teenagers get a driver's permit, they are not ready to drive. Before they step on the gas, they have to learn the rules of the road. They need to know basic information like how to turn a corner, how to pass someone, what the various speed limits are, and the meaning of road signs. Then, during a number of practice runs, the teen learns how to control the car, how to drive defensively, and how to do such maneuvers as parallel parking. After this training and practice the teen takes the state's written and driving tests. If the teen has sufficiently mastered the concepts and procedures, the state will issue a driver's license, after which the teen will be held responsible for following the rules and practicing safe driving.

Similar steps are needed for a parent to teach a child how to become a responsible human being, only the process takes place over a much longer period of time. The child starts out as a helpless infant, totally dependent on its parents—not ready to do anything on its own. As the child grows and develops, he or she is able to do more and more things independently. And as the child grows and begins to take on responsibility, he or she also needs to learn the consequences of irresponsibility.

> The American Association of Pediatrics states that an effective discipline strategy requires three important components: a positive, supportive and loving relationship between the parent(s) and child; use of positive reinforcement to increase desired behaviors; and applying punishment to reduce or eliminate undesired behaviors.

The process of shaping a child's behavior has ups and downs and takes hours and hours of "practice"—just like the many hours of practice it takes to learn how to parallel park successfully and to learn the rules of the road. For parents, this requires that they hold steady on the course and consistently administer proper discipline. Each mistake, even on the parents' side, could lengthen the process, just like getting too close to other parked cars can cause scrapes or dents that can be costly.

KIMBERLEE SAYS:

I was working with Ben, age 18, for some issues surrounding depression. Ben had been battling depression for a very long time and because of this, his parents have done many things for him. In their minds, they were lovingly helping him. What happened, though, was that this enabled Ben to continue in his depression and learn that he did not have to be proactive in his life.

When he finally came to see me, his parents were still waking him up for school and bugging him about his homework. He had learned to depend on others for most things. Ben had a lot of work to do in order to be responsible for his actions, but his parents had it equally hard. They had to learn that allowing Ben to be responsible and make mistakes was the wise and loving thing to do.

Things did improve after a significant amount of growing pains. Ben still has his own work to do, but he needed his parents to let go before he was able to start his own journey.

Once children begin to handle some responsibilities and freedoms, they will have ample opportunities to test the boundaries. In our driving illustration, this would be like teens with a new driver's license—now that they have the freedom to drive, will they also be responsible and follow the rules? Will they stop at the stoplight and stay within the speed limit? Some infringements can be fatal—they could run a stoplight and be hit by another car. Other infringements, like not signaling before turning, are minor and a little instruction or a gentle reminder is all that's needed.

Our friends, Tim and Darcy Kimmel, liken the various levels of infractions to misdemeanors or felonies and then determine the proper level of discipline based upon the severity of the behavior. A wise parent has to determine the severity of the infringement and the proper amount of discipline, similar to a police officer who determines if a traffic violation deserves a mere warning or a ticket.

The first step, however, is teaching the guidelines, and in the next chapter we will look at the principles involved in doing this.

STUDY QUESTIONS

Since each child is different, each will need different disciplining techniques. Think through the following questions:

1. In what ways are each of your children unique?

2. How will your disciplining techniques be tailored for each child?

3. How will you know if you have been too harsh or too lenient with your child?

4. Think about ways that you were disciplined by your parents. What were good elements that you want to include in your parenting? What are elements that you do not want to pass on to your children?

5. Gary Chapman has written a book on the five love languages, which include: 1) words of affirmation; 2) quality time;

3) receiving gifts; 4) acts of service; and 5) physical touch. Which love language applies best to each of your children?

6. Each child will have some combination of each of these, but it is important to know how to show your child love, especially when you have to discipline him. Given your child's unique make-up and nature, what would be the best way to show him love after you have had to discipline him?

TIME TO PRACTICE

Think about the best way to handle the following situation:

A five-year-old boy has never played video games because his parents do not feel it is something he should do. This child is playing at the neighbor's house, where video games are permitted. The boy's father goes over to get him for dinner and sees that he is playing a video game. He immediately grabs his child's arms and swats him on the behind. The little boy, with tears in his eyes, asks what he did wrong.

Do you think that the parent handled this situation appropriately? Did his actions follow the guidelines that God has laid out for us in Proverbs? If not, what should the father have done instead?

3

A Wise Parent Instructs – Teaching the Guidelines

Learning is not attained by chance; it must be sought for with ardor and attended to with diligence.

—ABIGAIL ADAMS
WIFE OF PRESIDENT JOHN ADAMS

The first time I took my young son out to teach him to play basketball he must have thought we were playing soccer because all he wanted to do was to kick the ball around. After a while I realized we were getting nowhere and that we'd probably had enough fun for one day.

About a year later I tried again, and this time it turned out to be a game of chase. About six months later I got him to hold the ball and then throw it toward the basket. I say "toward the basket," because if you didn't know where he was attempting to throw it, you would never know where it was supposed to be going. After a few fruitless attempts, his interest faded and we'd both had enough. About a year after that, he was able to dribble the ball, but his attempts at shooting still needed work.

Today my son is a decent basketball player, but to reach that level it took time and effort for him to learn the rules of the game and gain the necessary hand-eye coordination.

In many respects this is how children learn to follow rules. At first they have no clue about what they are supposed to do. Children basically start off making their own rules. In fact, they are a rule unto themselves—anything they want is theirs. If they don't get what they want, they cry until they do. A toddler's worldview goes something like this:

1. If I like it, it's mine.
2. If it's in my hand, it's mine.
3. If I can take it from you, it's mine.
4. If I had it a little while ago, it's mine.
5. If it's mine, it must never appear to be yours in any way.
6. If I'm doing or building something, all the pieces are mine.
7. If it looks just like mine, it's mine.
8. If I saw it first, it's mine.
9. If you are playing with something and you put it down, it automatically becomes mine.
10. If it's broken, it's yours.

KIMBERLEE SAYS:

Amanda, age 18, came to me for several issues, one of them being a lack of responsibility. Her mother made all of her appointments and paid for the sessions. Amanda shared that she was tired of her parents interfering with her life. So when Amanda missed one of the appointments her mother had made, I asked her parents to let Amanda pay for it. This was a natural way for Amanda to learn about taking responsibility and about consequences. It worked perfectly: Amanda apologized, made her next appointment, and paid her mother back. From then on she made amazing gains as she responded to counseling.

Children become frustrated when they don't get their own way, and parents get tired from constantly having to remind their children of the need for cooperation and kindness to others. These are hard lessons to learn at first, but as children grow and practice these graces, they improve at them and gradually begin to learn to get along with others.

Parenting is a long-term commitment with successes, failures, and lapses. At times it seems like our kids have never listened to us; at other times we have good reason to be proud of them. And these may both be on the same day!

> Discipline should be instructive and age-appropriate and should include positive reinforcement for good behavior. Punishment is only one aspect of discipline, and in order to be effective, it must be prompt, consistent, and fair.

Where Do Parents Begin?

Wise parents begin by teaching the guidelines. When Proverbs uses the Hebrew word *mûsar* ("discipline") it encompasses both *teaching* and *correcting*, and it is this level of discipline that should be used more than any other. It is designed to help parents in one of their primary roles: to teach appropriate behavior, inform of inappropriate behavior, and help their child to foresee possible negative consequences.

LEVEL 1: TEACHING THE GUIDELINES

Three principles of discipline fall under Level 1:

1. Teach appropriate behavior
2. Inform of improper behavior
3. Explain the negative consequences of disobedience

Although each of these principles is distinct, they tend to flow back and forth between each other when it comes to everyday parenting. For instance, your grade-school son is angry and blurts out a cuss word. You *inform* him that his word choice is inappropriate and you take the time to give him an example (*teach*) of what he could acceptably say when he's frustrated and angry. If the situation seems right, you may also *explain* how easy it is to fall into a habit of using inappropriate language, especially when angry, and how hurtful these words can be in our relationships. Thus, it's possible that in a given situation you might use all three of the following principles of discipline at this level.

Principle 1: Teach Appropriate Behavior

*A wise parent acts as an instructor and
teaches a child to behave appropriately.*

We all know that children don't automatically gravitate toward good behavior. Take manners for instance. Children aren't born knowing that they should say "please" and "thank you." Manners, like all good behavior, have to be taught.

Parents can teach appropriate behavior in three main ways: 1) by stating expectations in positive terms; 2) by encouragement; and 3) by modeling.

Accentuate the Positive

The book of Proverbs commonly states behavioral expectations in positive terms.

> My child, listen to me and treasure my instructions. Tune your ears to wisdom, and concentrate on understanding. Cry out for insight and understanding. Search for them as you would for lost money or hidden treasure. Then you will understand what it means to fear the LORD, and you will gain knowledge of God (2:1–5).

> Happy is the person who finds wisdom and gains understanding. For the profit of wisdom is better than silver, and her wages

are better than gold. Wisdom is more precious than rubies; nothing you desire can compare with her (3:13–15).[1]

The key to this level of discipline is to start early. Even toddlers can start learning appropriate behavior. At this age children are prone to hit, bite, or pull hair when frustrated, often because they are so limited in what they are able to say. Stating in positive terms what is appropriate is the place to start. The young child should be encouraged to "use your words" and "be gentle with your hands." Just know that in the early development stages, progress can be slow and require your frequent attention.

As children grow, giving positive choices can circumvent misbehavior. If your younger child wants to watch television more than you'd like, head them off with other choices. "Would you like to color or use Play-Doh right now?" limits the amount of their television viewing while at the same time encourages other interests.

As a child gets older, it is helpful to make statements you can reinforce, like "I serve breakfast to children who have made their bed" or "I'll listen when your voice is calm like mine." Statements like these put expectations in positive terms.

Your teen-agers can learn your curfew expectations with a statement like "You will show me that you are responsible by coming home on time." Then talk about how late they expect to be out. If they give a time that is later than you'd like, find out why they want stay out so late. Ideally, through dialogue you can come to an agreement on curfew for that night.

Offer Encouragement

Although no one looks forward to discipline, Proverbs encourages us to see it as a demonstration of God's love for us:

---

1. For additional references, see Proverbs 1:8-9; 2:1-22; 3:1-35; 4:1-13; 5:1-2; 6:20-26; 7:1-5; 8:1-36; 23:24-25.

My child, don't ignore it when the LORD disciplines you, and don't be discouraged when he corrects you. For the LORD corrects those he loves, just as a father corrects a child in whom he delights (3:11–12).

But it's easy to fall into a discouragement trap with our kids. They misbehave, we lash out with "no"... "don't you dare do that again"... "you'd better stop." Before we know it, we're saying "no" and "don't" all day long.

This happens to teachers as well. In *The Friendship Factor*, author Alan Loy McGinnis tells about the teacher of a second-grade class who complained that the class was getting harder and harder to control. Instead of listening and doing their work, the children would get up and wander around the class. Two psychologists were called in to see if anything could be done.

[The] psychologists spent several days at the back of the room with stopwatches, carefully observing the behavior of both the children and the teacher. Every ten seconds they recorded on their pads how many children were out of their seats. On average, some child was standing 360 times in every 20-minute period and the teacher said "Sit down!" 7 times in every 20-minute period.

The psychologists suggested that she consciously increase the number of times she commanded "Sit down!" and see what would happen. So in the next few days, according to observers, she yelled, "Sit down!" an average of 27.5 times per 20 minute period. Did that change the children's behavior? Indeed it did. They were out of their seats 540 times per period, or an increase of 50%...

Here is the kicker. For the final week, the researchers asked that the teacher refrain entirely from yelling "Sit down!" and instead quietly compliment children who were staying in their seats doing their work. The result? The roaming about decreased by 33%, the best behavior for the entire experiment.

What these psychologists suggested is called "proximal praise" and can be used in your home. As an example: One of your sons has a hard time sharing. When this happens, notice who is sharing and compliment that child: "Andy, you are doing such a great job sharing with Ethan!" Your other little guy is going to want to get the same compliment, and when he does share, compliment him immediately: "Oh, Ethan, you did such a nice job sharing!" The key is to make sure you compliment your child when he does what you want him to do.

KIMBERLEE SAYS:

I used to facilitate groups for children with attention deficit hyperactivity disorder (ADHD), mood disorders, and social skill issues. These children would find it very easy to get off task or would easily become frustrated with each other. Using proximal praise (praising a child who is doing what is asked, so that the child that is off-task can hear and turn their behavior around) was like having magic words. It worked so well that most of the time these children would change their focus on misbehaving into behaving so they could instantly receive positive feedback. I could not have run my groups any other way.

A good rule of thumb is to say "yes" whenever you can, but "no" when necessary.

My wife and I stumbled onto the power of encouragement when one of our sons was in early grade school. Back then there were periods when it seemed like we scolded him about one thing or another all day long. It became a vicious, negative cycle and, frankly, we got tired of scolding. So we decided to back off and instead make some encouraging comments whenever he did something right. Guess what? It broke the cycle of his misbehavior. It was amazing to watch his discouragement lift.

Our children need us to notice when they do things right.

> Positive reinforcement is crucial to discipline. One of the most powerful forms of positive reinforcement is parental attention, which should focus on good behavior rather than undesirable behavior. Unfortunately, undesirable behavior more frequently gains parental attention.

Modeling

The book of Proverbs also includes instruction on how important modeling is to the learning process, as these proverbs indicate:

My children, listen to me. Listen to your father's instruction. Pay attention and grow wise, for I am giving you good guidance. Don't turn away from my teaching. For I, too, was once my father's son, tenderly loved by my mother as an only child. My father told me, "Take my words to heart. Follow my instructions and you will live" (4:1–4).

Follow the steps of good men instead, and stay on the paths of the righteous. For only the upright will live in the land, and those who have integrity will remain in it (2:20–21).

We can be told principles over and over, but they remain abstract until we see them demonstrated in someone's life. They say a picture is worth a thousand words, and seeing something modeled in someone's life is a picture of that principle in action.

Being a consistent role model for your children is a daunting task, but God can help you to be the kind of model you need to be. Ask Him for help. When you blow it, ask Him for forgiveness and then move on, and through His help attempt to be the kind of model that He wants you to be.

KIMBERLEE SAYS:

Mary and Robert had two children, ages 3 and 8. After Mary and Robert divorced, Robert married Susan. Susan was very rude to Mary in front of the children. In one of our counseling sessions, the eight-year-old asked me why Susan was so mean to his mom, when his mom was nice to Susan. In talking with Mary about this, she told me that indeed Susan was not very nice to her in front of the kids. Susan would call her names and yell at her. Mary understood how important it was that her children saw her being kind to Susan and not feeding into Susan's poor behavior and attitude. Mary also said she made sure the children saw that she did not allow Susan to berate her in front of them and demonstrated boundaries. For instance, if Susan was being unpleasant, Mary would say, "It sounds like you are having a rough day. We can talk about this later"; or, "If you cannot be calm and talk to me nicely, this conversation can wait."

We need to model the kinds of behavior we expect from our children. Just by living with us our children see what we eat, how we spend our time, and our attitudes toward our neighbors. Even the way we drive can demonstrate a lot to our children. If we are impatient, cut people off, or shout at other drivers, we are teaching our children that this is appropriate behavior. A little voice from the back seat saying "Mommy (or Daddy) shouldn't have said that" may remind us when our actions don't match what we have told our children.

Most of what we teach our children about appropriate behavior takes place spontaneously when we spend time with them. Spending time is one of the best ways to show our love and model behavior.

KIMBERLEE SAYS:

Tim, age 7, had a mother who was always yelling at him. She asked me for help in relating to her son. I quickly realized that I would need to model appropriate discipline for her to learn from, as "theory" did not work with her. When Tim would do something that was not appropriate, I firmly but gently talked to him about his choices. I helped him process what he had done and what choice he could make next time. When he did make a better choice, I praised him. After observing this, Tim's mother soon implemented the discipline she saw me use with him.

In talking more with Tim's mother, I learned that she did not have great parenting examples when she was growing up; she was using what had been used on her. She did not know any other way to parent. She agreed that it did not work for her, and that she now saw that it did not work with her son.

Charles Francis Adams, a nineteenth-century political figure and diplomat, one day wrote in his diary: "Went fishing with my son today—a day wasted." His son, Brook Adams, also kept a diary. On that same day, Brook Adams made this entry: "Went fishing with my father—the most wonderful day of my life!" These journal entries reveal the marked contrast between the two different motivations: the father was spending time with his son out of duty, but the son longed to be with his father and valued every moment.

When one of my sons was young, he loved to go to the park and swing. We'd see how high we could go and watch the cars go by at the same time. He could have done that for hours. I remember how hard it was finding time to do this with my son, but I knew he loved it and I knew it was important to spend time with him. We chatted as we walked to the park and as we swung. Now, those are some of my fondest memories of his childhood.

As children grow up, we demonstrate our love for them in many different ways, all of which involve time. This past spring my wife and I realized that before long our sons will be heading off to college and moving out on their own. We saw the need to talk with them about godly values and other things we consider important. I decided to take hikes with my sons on a regular basis and use that time to enjoy their company and talk with them about such things as: What makes good friends? What goals do they have for their lives? What do they remember about growing up? My wife found that driving with them on errands or to activities was a great time to chat and to talk about important things.

Spending time getting to know your children is also good for you as a parent. I remember when one of my sons was "going through a stage." He was often moody, uncooperative, and hard to please. I found it difficult to feel close to him. But I decided to try and spend more time with him, and as I did, he began to change. But an even bigger change came over me—I started to feel closer and more connected with him.

If our children don't know that we love them unconditionally, no matter what they do or how they act, then it's hard for them to respond properly to our discipline.

Points to Remember

1. Explain your expectations of appropriate behavior in positive terms.
2. Encouragement is a powerful tool for shaping young lives. Use it often.

3. Our lives constantly model behavior. Make sure you are modeling the message you want to be sending.
4. If you spend more time encouraging good behavior, you may be able to spend less time dealing with inappropriate behavior.
5. Parenting takes time. We need to *be* with our children if we are to teach and model appropriate behavior for them.

John Rosemead, a family psychologist, says, "In the good old days (and make no mistake about it, while certainly not idyllic, they were far better), parents concentrated their energies on shaping character. They were intent upon raising children who embodied the Three R's of respect, responsibility, and resourcefulness. Today's parents, by contrast, seek to raise children who possess high self-esteem, which researchers have found is correlated highly with low tolerance for frustration, low self-control, and a sense of personal entitlement. Be careful what you wish for, eh?

Principle 2 : Inform of Improper Behavior

A wise parent is proactive and addresses issues before the child might be confronted by them.

It's always wise to head off trouble before it starts. For instance, you're going to take your daughter into the front yard to play ball for the first time. She's very excited, and you know that if the ball heads into the road, she'll probably want to run after it. So you tell her, before it even happens, that the ball might go into the road. If it does, she can't go get it. By anticipating and instructing, eventually you will teach your daughter how to check to see if it's safe to enter the road and get the ball. Later, as she gains more independence, you need to teach her about "stranger danger." And when she is a new driver, she needs to understand that blaring radios, cell phones, and too many passengers in the car are huge and dangerous distractions while she is driving.

These are all basic safety issues that we teach our children to help protect them. But what about helping our children avoid other kinds of trouble? Proverbs gives parents guidance on that.

KIMBERLEE SAYS:

So many of my clients' parents share with me that they spank their children for every little infraction. They really believe this is the best way to curb behavior. It makes me so sad that there is very little dialogue, just spanking. Most of the parents confess that they hit in anger, and some are remorseful for doing this, but do not know any other way.

The book of Proverbs—in fact, all of Scripture—anticipates wrong attitudes and behavior and informs us what those are so that we can avoid them. Proverbs 6:16–19 states:

There are six things the Lord hates—no, seven things he detests:

> haughty eyes,
> a lying tongue,
> hands that kill the innocent,
> a heart that plots evil,
> feet that race to do wrong,
> a false witness who pours out lies,
> a person who sows discord among brothers. [2]

---

2. For additional Proverbs covering these themes see: Proverbs 1:10-19; 4:14-27; 6:1-19; 7:6-21; 9:13-18; 22:24-25; 23:26-28.

Another example of a proverb that warns of the dangers of inappropriate behavior in a convincing way is Proverbs 5:15–18:

> Drink water from your own well—share your love only with your wife. Why spill the water of your springs in public, having sex with just anyone? You should reserve it for yourselves. Don't share it with strangers.
>
> Let your wife be a fountain of blessing for you. Rejoice in the wife of your youth.

Not only is this a creative description of purity and fidelity in marriage, but it also leaves a strong image in the mind of the reader.

In these and other verses we are told explicitly that God disapproves of certain behavior, and it is done in a neutral context before the start of the behavior, not in the middle of it. And because we have been informed and warned by God the Father, we may be able to avoid some of the sins that are mentioned. He gives us the opportunity to modify our wrong behavior.

Our children need to know that there are certain things they shouldn't do; they need to know that there are limits and boundaries in life.

Setting limits is difficult but no one ever said parenting was an easy task. Parents must set limits for their children. No one else can discipline with the same love, affection, and concern as a parent. When kids know where the limits are, they feel safe.

Let's Apply It

To anticipate behavioral issues, you must know your children and what their typical responses tend to be. Does your child have a hard time sharing her toys when a friend comes to play? Talk with her about the importance of sharing before her next play session. Decide if there are favorite toys that should be put away. Explain to your child why not sharing is unacceptable. Help your child decide on some activities she would like to do with her friends when they play together.

> Explain the rules before a child breaks one, not afterward. Speak at the child's level (heads even) and make eye contact. Check for understanding by saying, "Tell me the rule." Don't ever ask, "Do you understand?"

Does your child have a meltdown in the grocery store when he sees candy or other favorite items? There are a variety of things you can do to stop this manipulative behavior. Your child needs to be told that tantrums in the store are not acceptable. On a positive note, give your child some choices. Tell him, for instance, that he can help choose the cereal, the soup, and the crackers. But when he decides to test your resolve with a tantrum, have a plan of action. Scoop him up, tell him firmly "No," and then leave the store if he doesn't stop throwing the tantrum. This may be inconvenient for you in terms of getting groceries that day, but in the long run you will have a more cooperative child for future shopping runs. Of course, a child who is tired, hungry, or has been shuffled around all day will be easily frustrated and have little self-control.

A mother of three young children told me about one way that she helps them avoid inappropriate behavior. Whenever her children are invited to a friend's party, on the way to the party while they are still in the van, she talks through with her children how she expects them to respond and what would be inappropriate to say.

"If you receive a present you already have, don't complain and say you wished you had been given something else. Instead, take it and say thank you. Or if you're given something to eat that you don't like, go ahead and eat a little of it without complaining, or at least politely say thank you for the food." This wise mother knows that kids don't have mature social graces and tend to say just what's on their mind. She helps them think through in advance problem situations, and tells them what responses to avoid and what responses would be acceptable.

KIMBERLEE SAYS:

Jordan, age 12, has Attention Deficit Hyperactivity Disorder (ADHD). She and her parents often argued over daily activities such as getting up in the morning, homework, talking too long on the phone. Her parents warned her that if she could do things on her own, they would not argue; but if they had to remind her all the time to do certain things, the consequence was an argument and often times punishments.

Jordan and I worked on a schedule/chart that she could keep in a place that she would see all the time. This chart had a list of things she needed to get done. She also bought a vibrating alarm watch that she would set when she was on the phone so she would not talk too long. When Jordan followed the chart and used her watch, she and her parents had fewer arguments. Jordan and her parents loved this new system, and Jordan learned the wisdom of responsibility.

With older children, use teaching opportunities that come up naturally. If a friend of your teenage daughter gets pregnant, talk about what life will be like for her friend and what would be the best ways to help her. Talk about how your daughter could avoid becoming pregnant herself—and be specific about what situations she might find herself in. Brainstorm about what she can do in those situations and/or how to avoid them.

If your teenage son is invited to a party, talk about your expectations and the kinds of things that can happen at teenage parties. Find out if there will be adult supervision. Discuss what to do if his friends drink or decide to use drugs, how to know when to leave if necessary, and what he should do if he needs a ride. Discuss curfew and what will happen if he's not back in time. Make sure he knows your expectations about inappropriate behavior, and make sure he knows you trust him unless he gives you reason not to.

One of the best possible learning experiences happened when our son got his first job. He learned about the importance of getting to work on time, how to deal with other people, how to work with a willing attitude and hundreds of other important lessons. When they enter the workplace, teenagers need to learn that you don't call in sick when you aren't, you don't talk on your cell phone at work, and you don't steal even the smallest item from the store or office or factory.

Talking about all of these things before they ever happen may save your child from some serious consequences.

Points to Remember

1. Inform your children of improper behavior in a neutral context, not when they are in the midst of it.
2. Instruct, don't emote. Teachers don't yell instructions to their students.
3. Teach your children what words to use in certain situations, and what actions are appropriate.
4. Make sure the guidelines are clear and understood. By talking about what constitutes improper behavior in advance of a situation, you will stop that common complaint, "You never told me I couldn't do that."

5. Vary the way you inform your children about improper behavior. When teaching moments present themselves, use them to their fullest potential. If a picture is worth a thousand words, then a good example of improper behavior and its consequences will provide strong incentives to do the right thing.

Principle 3: Explain the Negative Consequences of Disobedience

A wise parent points out the negative consequences of sinful behaviors that are frequently encountered in life.

One cold winter morning in Iowa when I was a kid, several of us eight-year-old boys came up with the bright idea of sticking our tongues on the jungle gym bars during recess. I didn't want to do it, but the other guys called me chicken, so of course I had to show them I wasn't. I stuck my warm tongue on the cold surface. And just like the tongues of the hundreds of kids before me, it stuck to the freezing metal. Since I didn't want to stay there for the rest of recess, I pulled it off, leaving a layer of skin behind. I learned that consequence the hard way.

Someone has said, "Experience is knowing a lot of things you shouldn't do." We as parents have learned many things in life the hard way—things we'd avoid if we had the chance to do life over again. Wouldn't it be great to pass on some of this wisdom to our children so that they, hopefully, might learn from our experience?

The book of Proverbs refers often to this principle of discipline,[3] and the authors explain the negative consequences of sin without mincing words. For example, "Don't lust for her [the adulteress] beauty. Don't let her coyness seduce you. For a prostitute will bring you to poverty, and sleeping with another man's wife may cost you your very life" (Proverbs 6:25–26).

---

3. For additional references, see: Proverbs 1:10-33; 5:1-23; 6:26-35; 7:22-27; 9:17-18; 10:1; 13:18; 14:14; 16:18, 26; 17:20; 18:13; 23:10-12; 24:17-20.

The authors are also creative in conveying the dangers of certain life choices: "Can a man scoop fire into his lap and not be burned? Can he walk on hot coals and not blister his feet?" (Proverbs 6:27–28). The young man who may be tempted to think there are few consequences to adultery or casual sex or linking up with a prostitute now has a vivid warning—these things can burn you, impoverish you, or end your life early.

Note the urgency in the author's desire to unmask the seductiveness of sin by describing its negative consequences, which helps us to see sin for what it really is. For example, look at what Proverbs has to say about using illegal means to get ahead in life:

> My child, if sinners entice you, turn your back on them! They may say, "Come and join us. Let's hide and kill someone! Let's ambush the innocent!... Come on, throw in your lot with us; we'll split our loot with you."
>
> Don't go along with them, my child! Stay far away from their paths. They rush to commit crimes.... They set an ambush for themselves; they booby-trap their own lives! Such is the fate of all who are greedy for gain. It ends up robbing them of life (1:10–11, 14, 15–16, 18–19).

Do you see how the author shows that this get-rich-quick scheme, which sounds so good, will at some point backfire and the sinners will get caught? It is another way of saying: if it sounds too good to be true, it probably is.

God expects parents to warn their children of behavior that can easily pull them in—things that look so good but have long-lasting negative consequences. Things that we may be tempted to think no one will ever know about.

If parents don't warn their children about these dangers, then who will? Children don't have enough life experience to know when things are not as good as they sound.

Initially a child believes behaviors are right or wrong because you tell her so, or she considers the consequences. By five years of age your child begins to internalize your values: what's right for you becomes right for her. Your values, virtuous or not, become part of your child.

Between seven and ten the child enters the age of moral reasoning. Now the child begins to act right because it is the right thing to do. By seven years of age, most children have developed their concept of "what's normal." If sensitivity, caring, politeness, and empathy have been standard operating procedure in the child's home, those are his norms, and he operates according to them. What his parents take seriously, the child takes seriously. Up to this point, he believes his parents to be infallible, so he enters middle childhood with their values as part of himself.

Let's Apply It

When teaching children to foresee negative consequences, take into account what is developmentally appropriate. The young child does not have a concept of time and lives in the present, so putting a toy away for an hour or so is a sufficiently long consequence. About age five, a child will probably understand the difference between past, present, and future. But it's not until age seven or eight that children are able to understand what a "few days' time" is.

Older kids have a hard time seeing how what they do now could affect their lives for years to come. And it doesn't make it any easier that our culture has become so "in the moment." Lots of adults fall into the trap of "enjoy now, pay later."

It is so easy to think we'll be the one to get away without a scratch, no damage done. We tend to think we'll be able to avoid any long-term consequences, and it can lead us to take unwise risks, as Ron Hutchcraft highlights in his book *Wake Up Calls*:

> In 1982, "ABC Evening News" reported on an unusual work of modern art—a chair affixed to a shotgun. It was to be viewed by sitting in the chair and looking directly into the gun barrel. The gun was loaded and set on a timer to fire at an undetermined moment within the next hundred years. The amazing thing was that people waited in lines to sit and stare into the shell's path! They all knew the gun could go off at point-blank range at any moment, but they were gambling that the fatal blast wouldn't happen during *their* minute in the chair. Yes, it was foolhardy, yet many people who wouldn't dream of sitting in that chair live a lifetime gambling that they can get away with sin. Foolishly they ignore the risk until the inevitable self-destruction.

There is also the fact that many things just aren't considered sin any more. Instead, people tend to talk about a "little mistake," a "weakness," or a "problem." Few things are so bad that they are called "sin." Or, they say, "It's nothing that I couldn't walk away from today if I wanted to." Thus, repeated sin can become a pattern, a habit, an addiction that is difficult to break. We liken it to the way an Eskimo kills a wolf:

> First, the Eskimo coats his knife blade with animal blood and allows it to freeze. Then he adds another layer of blood, and another, until the blade is completely concealed by frozen blood. Next, the hunter fixes his knife in the ground with the blade up. When a wolf follows his sensitive nose to the source of the scent and discovers the bait, he licks it, tasting the fresh frozen blood. He begins to lick faster, more and more vigorously, lapping the blade until the keen edge is bare. Feverishly now, harder and harder, the wolf licks the blade in the arctic night.

So great becomes his craving for blood that the wolf does not notice the razor-sharp sting of the naked blade on his own tongue, nor does he recognize the instant at which his insatiable thirst is being satisfied by his own warm blood. His carnivorous appetite just craves more—until the dawn finds him dead in the snow!"

Like the wolf that doesn't notice the sting on his tongue, repeated sin dulls our conscience. We give in more easily and indulge more often until it becomes a regular part of our life.

Along with the importance of teaching long-term consequences, Proverbs also teaches us to recognize the danger signs in certain situations. For example:

The woman approached him, dressed seductively and sly of heart. She was the brash, rebellious type who never stays at home. She is often seen in the streets and markets, soliciting at every corner.

She threw her arms around him and kissed him, and with a brazen look she said,... my husband is not home. He's away on a long trip...

So she seduced him with her pretty speech. With her flattery she enticed him. He followed her at once, like an ox going to the slaughter, or like a trapped stag (7:10–13, 19, 21–22).

What is the implication for parents? We should teach our children that sometimes they need to leave a situation quickly, before their good judgment gets clouded and they make the wrong choice.

The other implication is that we need to be just as frank with our children about sex as the book of Proverbs is. The media freely gives them input on sex. Their friends do as well. So why, as Herbert Wagemaker asks in *Parents and Discipline*, is premarital pregnancy so often the first conversation about sex between parents and children?

In *Homemade*, Dr. Richard Dobbins uses the image of adhesive tape to demonstrate the importance of sexual purity:

> Adhesive tape is not made for repetitive use. The strongest bond adhesive tape is capable of making is formed with the first surface to which it is applied. You can remove the tape and reapply it to other surfaces several times, and it will still adhere. However, with every application, some of the adhesiveness has been compromised. Finally, if you continue the practice long enough, there will not be enough adhesiveness left to make the tape stick to any surface. God intended that the bond between mates be the closest and strongest one they are capable of forming. That is why Paul makes it very clear that the body is not for fornication.

KIMBERLEE SAYS:

Amber, 17, prided herself on being a virgin when she came to see me the first time. During our time together, she started dating a boy she really liked. She told me they were going to get married after they finished college. With that thought in her mind, she gave her most precious gift to him, her virginity. A few months after that, they broke up. After that, Amber had sex with a few more men and told me it was "no big deal anymore."

Her parents do not know about the decisions Amber has made. They just assumed she would remain a virgin since Amber was a compliant young woman.

Important issues to discuss with your younger children could be sharing, getting along with others, telling the truth, being kind, helping others, not stealing, not hurting others; but as your children get older, you will need to talk with them about issues like pornography and other temptations.

The key to getting our children to hear us on these important issues is our rapport with them. Nagging is not an effective teaching tool. Look for "teachable moments"—those wonderful opportunities that arise naturally but can pass in a moment if we miss them. And sometimes we will need to intentionally create opportunities to talk to our kids about serious concerns such as how to treat others, manners, what makes a good friend, college, finances, dating, future goals, what they are looking for in a spouse, sex, marriage, family life, and divorce.

Parents need wisdom to balance the right amount of information with the age of the child. Just don't be naïve—elementary school children are exposed to a whole lot more than their parents were at that age.

Even more schools are starting to teach morals as an important part of a student's education. "Conscience is like a muscle," Twal said. "We either practice it and it grows, or it atrophies. What I do in my classroom is to give students an opportunity to exercise their conscience. I want to develop character, not self-esteem. . . . I think the greatest disservice that we have done to our kids is to tell them they are okay the way they are."

We can teach the guidelines, but when our children make mistakes (and they will) we can re-teach by helping them see and understand what happened.

As our children get older, we need more and more wisdom to help them (and ourselves) through the difficult situations. Remember that James 1:5 says, "If any of you lacks wisdom, let him ask of God, who gives to all generously and without reproach, and it will be given to him" (NASB). Thank God that He wants to give us great wisdom, for we all need it.

One area that we needed to talk through with our son was how friends can sway us toward wrong attitudes and behavior. My son seemed to gravitate toward friends who would boss him around. If they told him to jump, he jumped. He needed to learn to look for more equal friendships—more equal give and take. He needed to learn the importance of choosing his friends wisely and understanding that the wrong friends could influence him to act in negative ways.

KIMBERLEE SAYS:

The issue with friends is a very common concern parents have when they bring their children in for counseling. Teaching your children when they are young about how to choose friends wisely is essential to avoid this issue when they are teens. When they are teens it becomes much more serious.

Points to Remember
1. Warn your children about the consequences of sin. If you don't, who will?
2. Think of creative ways to picture the negative aspects of sin (think of Proverbs) so that your children will want to flee from it.
3. Share your own mistakes. This may save them some heartaches in their lives

Parents are the most influential instructors children have, and they either succeed or fail based upon their ability to be consistent, loving, and wise. Each situation brings new challenges, and there are many times that parents are tempted to give up. Encouraging and loving your children is the best way to get them through life's rough spots with the fewest number of catastrophes. Remember, you have to encourage, demonstrate, and model a godly lifestyle.

Things to Try

1. Spend time with your children, as a family and with each child individually. Have a family movie night, go ice skating, shopping, or out for ice cream. I took my boys on hikes during the summer and tried to have a special topic we could talk about on each of the hikes, like what makes a good friend, what is a good use of our finances, or girls.

2. Try to get your children to think about appropriate boundaries, whether it is with their friends or with the opposite sex. What should they do if their friend tries to get them to do something they know, or suspect, is wrong? When they go out on dates, what are their boundaries? It is not easy to get kids to sit down and talk about boundaries. Sometimes a good way to approach it is to come at it from another direction: for example, start with problems their friends might be having with their dates.

3. Encourage your children for acting properly. When children are young, they need constant encouragement. It might be helpful to keep a list on the refrigerator recording each of the times the child has done a good job on something. When the page gets full, give the child a special treat. As children get older, parents tend to think that this is no longer necessary, but that is not true. Do you no longer need encouragement? Think of ways verbally to encourage your children at least once a day.

KIMBERLEE SAYS:

Sandra, 15, was brought into my office by her mother, Debra. Debra was frustrated that her daughter was pulling away from her and not wanting to spend any time with her. I encouraged Debra to set weekly time with Sandra and do something that Sandra would like to do. Debra did this for one week. She then told me that Sandra did not want to do it any more. This was perplexing, so I asked Sandra what happened. Sandra explained that when her mother asked her what she wanted to do, Sandra told her she wanted to go to the library to get some books and then go for ice cream. When asked if they did that, Sandra explained that her mother told her that was boring and to think of something better to do. This crushed Sandra and, needless to say, she refused to think of any other things they might do. Once Debra was coached on how to talk with her daughter, and how to listen without being critical, and how to validate her feelings, their relationship began to improve.

4. Develop the habit of sitting down with your child right before bedtime and helping them think through their day. What are things that the child did well? What are things that he or she would like to improve upon tomorrow or in the future?

STUDY QUESTIONS

1. What are some of the ways that a parent can teach a child what is appropriate behavior?

2. Keep a log for the next two weeks to see how you are responding to your children. Describe each situation where discipline was used. How did you respond? What did you teach your child through your response? Did you apply a consistent method of discipline? What would you change if you encounter that situation again?

3. Go through the book of Proverbs and find verses that teach about certain topics (e.g., wise use of money, the importance of purity, watching your words). List five key topics and then find proverbs you could use to teach these to your children.

   1. Topic:
      Proverbs:
   2. Topic:
      Proverbs:
   3. Topic:
      Proverbs:
   4. Topic:
      Proverbs:
   5. Topic:
      Proverbs:

4. Use the book of Proverbs for your devotions for a few months and see if there are ways to share your insights with your children. Sometimes specific proverbs can deal with difficult issues in a clear, non-threatening way.

TIME TO PRACTICE

How would you respond to the following situation?

You, your spouse, and your children are on your way to church and you are running late. You are driving. You may be tempted to speed, yell at the other drivers to get out of your way, or a variety of other impatient reactions. What would be a better way to handle this and what could you do next week to make sure that this does not happen again?

4

A Wise Parent Warns— Reiterating the Guidelines

One timely cry of warning can save nine of surprise.
—JOSHUA THOMPSON

Imagine having a child who has never learned that there are boundaries. That child would be uncontrollable, as the following story from James Dobson's book *New Dare to Discipline* illustrates:

> I once dealt with a mother of a rebellious thirteen-year-old boy who snubbed every hint of parental authority. He would not come home until at least two o'clock in the morning, and deliberately disobeyed every request she made of him. Assuming that her lack of control was a long-standing difficulty, I asked if she would tell me the history of this problem. She clearly remembered when it all started: Her son was less than three at the time. She carried him to his room and placed him in his crib, and he spit in her face.
>
> She explained the importance of not spitting in mommy's face, but was interrupted by another moist missile. This mother had been told that all confrontations could be resolved by love, understanding, and discussion. So she wiped her face and began again, at which point she was hit with another well-aimed blast. Growing increasingly frustrated, she shook him... but not hard enough to disrupt his aim with the next wad.

What could she do then? Her philosophy offered no honorable solution to this embarrassing challenge. Finally, she rushed from the room in utter exasperation, and her little conqueror spat on the back of the door as it shut. She lost; he won! This exasperated mother told me she never had the upper hand with her child after that night!

It is inevitable that children will want to test the established rules or guidelines, which will call for some sort of discipline. At this point a wise parent has to make a decision as to the severity of the disobedience and what would be a reasonable punishment. When this happens, a parent may feel that they have failed or feel guilty that they need to use some form of punishment on their child. However, this is not the parent's fault and they need not feel guilty; the fault lies solely with the child and the choices that he or she is making.

All children misbehave at some time; it's part of finding out what appropriate behavior is and where the limits are. Children may throw tantrums, test the rules, start fights, refuse to cooperate with family routines, use bad language—the list goes on. As parents teach children appropriate behavior, what the expected rules and boundaries are all about, it's important to remember the goals of discipline. Discipline means helping a child develop self-control and a sense of limits, experience the consequences of his/her behavior, and learn from his/her mistakes.... All children need the security of knowing the rules and boundaries of behavior; without them they feel at a loss.

Principle: Give Appropriate Warnings

*A wise parent will warn a child
when a behavior needs to change.*

Warnings help us learn. You are driving in an unfamiliar neighborhood looking for a street when you see the squad car lights in your rearview mirror. You have no idea how fast you were going because you were preoccupied with finding your way. The officer who pulls you over decides to give you a warning instead of a ticket. You have been informed or reminded what the speed limit is, and now you have the chance to continue on again, this time hopefully choosing to stay within that limit.

In the same way, our kids need to be warned that they are at the boundary line between appropriate and inappropriate behavior. Maybe they don't realize their behavior is approaching or has even crossed over the line. Or maybe they know and want to find out if you notice, to test you to see if you'll enforce the rules. In either case, a warning tells your child when he or she needs to make a change.

When we see our children heading in the wrong direction, or starting to do something they should not do, they need our warning not to go further.

A number of verses in the book of Proverbs serve as a warning for what to do when you're in the middle of a situation, at the boundary line of behavior—one step more in the wrong direction will cause you to cross the line into sin.[1]

My child, if sinners entice you, turn your back on them (1:10).

Wisdom will save you from evil people, from those whose speech is corrupt (2:12).

---

1. See also: Proverbs 1:7, 15, 19, 22, 28, 31-33; 2:11-19, 22; 3:7, 11; 4:2, 5-6, 14-19, 23-27; 5:3-16, 21-23; 6:1-5, 9-15, 25-35; 7:24-27; 8:33-36; 9:13-18; 10:1-24:34; 26:17-29:27; 31:2-9.

Child misbehavior is impossible to prevent completely. Children, usually curious and endlessly creative, are likely to do things parents and other caregivers have not expected. However, there are many positive steps adults can take to help prevent misbehavior.

- Set clear, consistent rules.
- Make certain the environment is safe and worry-free.
- Show interest in the child's activities.
- Provide appropriate and engaging playthings.
- Encourage self-control by providing meaningful choices.
- Focus on the desired behavior, rather than the one to be avoided.
- Build children's images of themselves as trustworthy, responsible, and cooperative.
- Expect the best from the child.
- Give clear directions, one at a time.
- Say "Yes" whenever possible.
- Notice and pay attention to children when they do things right.
- Take action before a situation gets out of control.
- Encourage children often and generously.
- Set a good example.
- Help children see how their actions affect others.

The man who commits adultery is an utter fool, for he destroys his own soul (6:32).

Remember, sin can be very attractive, and it will often take an active decision on the part of your child to turn away from it. Part of the process at this level is reminding your child of what you have already told him or her.

> My son, obey your father's commands, and don't neglect your mother's teaching. Keep their words always in your heart. Tie them around your neck. Wherever you walk, their counsel can lead you. When you sleep, they will protect you. When you wake up in the morning, they will advise you. For these commands and this teaching are a lamp to light the way ahead of you. The correction of discipline is the way to life (6:20–23).

Notice that last sentence: "The correction of discipline is the way to life." Correction that comes from discipline is the path that leads to life.

> Follow my advice, my son; always treasure my commands. Obey them and live! Guard my teachings as your most precious possession. Tie them on your fingers as a reminder. Write them deep within your heart (7:1–3).

So what is the principle being taught here? First of all, that knowing what behavior is expected, knowing what is considered misbehavior, and knowing that misbehavior has negative consequences is a learning process. And second, in this learning process children need to be warned when they are in the "danger zone" with their behavior, when they are either getting close to misbehaving or have just acted inappropriately. If it is the first time you are dealing with this specific type of behavior, a warning without any additional consequences might be appropriate. This will give your child the chance to learn where the boundary line is.

Sometimes a warning is inherent in a proverb—a warning to live properly or in time sin will take its toll. For example:

> A wise child brings joy to a father; a foolish child brings grief to a mother (10:1).

71

We all have happy memories of the godly, but the name of a wicked person rots away (10:7).

Fear of the LORD lengthens one's life, but the years of the wicked are cut short (10:27).

Your own soul is nourished when you are kind, but you destroy yourself when you are cruel (11:17).

Evil people get rich for the moment, but the reward of the godly will last (11:18).

When adults make rules and stick to them, children feel safe and secure. But children often fight with their parents about rules. That is the "work" they do in order to learn about rules. Even though children may act like they want to be in charge, they really need adults to be in charge.

The "work" of parents is to stick to the rules. Sometimes your child will not like you for that. That is okay. At this time in your child's life, your child needs you to be a parent—not just a friend. Your child needs you to be firm but caring with rules. That is hard work and takes time. And at the end of a work day, it is hard for parents to find the energy for that.

Making rules is an important part of loving. When rules work, you help your child feel safe, loved, and able to get along with others.

And in some proverbs the consequence for not heeding the warning is explicitly stated:

I [wisdom] called you so often, but you didn't come. I reached out to you, but you paid no attention. You ignored my advice and rejected the correction I offered. So I will laugh when you are in trouble! I will mock you when disaster overtakes you...

I will not answer when they cry for help. Even though they anxiously search for me, they will not find me. For they hated knowledge and chose not to fear the LORD. They rejected my advice and paid no attention when I corrected them. That is why they must eat the bitter fruit of living their own way. They must experience the full terror of the path they have chosen (1:24–26, 28–31).

In this passage, wisdom sounds heartless, but when you see the whole context it makes sense. If we abandon wisdom and choose to go our own sinful path, there is nothing that wisdom can do for us. Basically it is saying that we get only one shot at living our life wisely. Once we start down the wrong path and make wrong choices, it will continue to lead to more wrong choices and in the end, destruction. After we have rejected the truth for so long, punishment must set in. In other words, at some point we will reap the consequences for all those years of living unwisely.

Let's Apply It

One of the first things we need to understand in applying this principle is that warning and nagging are two different things—and we want to avoid nagging.

Do you ever hear yourself saying, "If I've told you once, I've told you a hundred times"? It's easy for parents to get caught in a cycle like this, because it takes resolve and effort on our part to follow through after the warning stage.

However, giving repeated warnings isn't any more effective than nagging. Repeated warnings tend to sound something like this: "I'm warning you... don't make me come over there... if you don't stop right now..." and on, and on, until we blow a fuse and yell.

KIMBERLEE SAYS:

Monica came into our office with her two young boys. While they were sitting in the waiting room, Monica was texting on her cell phone and her boys were fighting. Every few minutes Monica would say, "Stop it you two!" or "Knock it off or else you will get into big trouble!" They stopped initially, and then started to giggle and provoked each other again and again. Monica never followed through with any discipline. She seemed to get more and more frustrated, but nothing ever got resolved. Monica was called into her appointment and left her two boys in the waiting room. Our staff had to ask the boys several times to be quiet, but the boys did not listen to our staff either. They had learned that they don't have to listen because apparently there were rarely consequences from their misbehavior.

We all fall into the trap of saying, "If you don't stop that right now, I'll…" without really backing it up. When our boys were younger, my wife got tired of reaching the yelling point. She realized one day that she was trying to "discipline from across the room" and it didn't work. A typical scenario went something like this: She'd be doing the dishes while the boys played in the adjoining family room. Eventually one boy would do something to irritate the other and they'd start fighting. Without stopping her work, she'd tell whoever she thought started it to stop. It worked—for a couple minutes. But then the fighting would begin all over again, and she'd end up yelling at them both from the kitchen.

My wife learned to stop what she was doing, walk over to the boys, look the offender in the eyes, and tell him in a calm, firm voice to stop. She also informed the offender of what he was doing wrong that needed to stop. Sometimes there were consequences (we'll talk about that in the next chapter). Before long the boys figured out that when Mom used her calm, quiet, firm voice she meant business.

We don't need to threaten and yell, but we do need to be firm.

We also need wisdom to evaluate whether the situation calls for a warning or for consequences. Remember, we can't expect perfection. Our child might not get it right the first time (or even the second time), but we all often need second chances.

> Some rules are non-negotiable, like "Don't drink and drive," but keep these to a minimum. Parents who make a major confrontation out of every minor issue risk losing all their influence with their teenagers. In demanding quiet submission, they may unwittingly create a simmering foe. Whenever possible, state rules as guidelines rather than ultimatums. Otherwise, family life will become a series of power struggles.
>
> Parents need to help their children make the transition from parental discipline to self-discipline. For this to happen, teens need to learn how to negotiate and how to cooperate in setting rules and solving problems. Today, as their horizons expand, teens are more often out of our sight; they need to learn how to think for themselves so they can make the right choices when parents are not around.

In the process of giving a warning, we can also give our child the opportunity to think of an appropriate consequence if he or she chooses to keep heading in the wrong direction. For example, you have asked your daughter to clean her room but she continues to play her video game. You give her a warning. If she can't tell time yet, set a timer and tell her that when the timer rings she needs to clean her room. If she can tell time, tell her what time her room needs to be clean. In either case, ask her what consequence there should be if she doesn't clean her room. Now that the boundary line between cooperation and misbehavior is clearly defined, she can make a choice, and you have a plan of action if she chooses not to cooperate.

When your children are older, continue using this same principle of warning and follow-through. Is your teenager just starting to go out at night and learning whether you will enforce curfews? If he stays out too late and it's the first time that has happened, give a warning—remind him what the consequences will be if it happens again. But also find out if there were extenuating circumstances— why he wasn't home on time. If it happens several times and he always has an excuse, you'll need to draw the boundary line more firmly by backing it up with consequences. (We'll talk more about consequences in the next chapter.)

Remember, the basic purpose for this level of discipline is to give the child one more chance to get it right. A warning may need to be emphasized by some form of non-corporal punishment, such as a time out, or the removal of a toy, a favorite object, or a privilege. As children get older we may need to remove a privilege, an allowance, or grounding may be necessary.

Warnings are intended to stop certain unacceptable behavior. We do this because we love our children and, ultimately, because this is for their own good.

KIMBERLEE SAYS:

Alexis was 6 when she came to see me. One of her issues was that she had quite a rebellious side to her. She was a sweet girl who helped out when she wanted to, but when her parents asked her to do something, she defiantly said "no" and continued to do whatever she was doing. They tried taking things away, time outs, and spanking, but nothing seemed to curb her behavior. What they were missing was the part about talking to Alexis about the importance of listening and following directions. While this can be a bit time-consuming, Alexis was a child who needed to know the "why" before she would do things.

For example, Alexis never wanted to put her toys away. I had her parents explain the importance of putting them away: "your toys won't get broken by someone stepping on them" ... "people won't get hurt because they won't trip over your toys" ... "if you show us that you can take care of your toys by putting them in their 'homes,' you are showing us that you can handle even more toys." I suggested that they then make a game out of it. See how fast she could put them away, or how neatly she could put them away. Regardless of how she did it, her parents were then to give her lots of praise for being a big girl and taking good care of her toys. And then when she did get a new toy, they were to let her know she really deserved it because she took care of her things. Methods like these worked for Alexis.

Points to Remember

1. A warning must be clear and must include what will happen if the warning is not heeded.
2. Warnings are necessary. God gives us warnings, but He is also very patient with us.
3. When issuing a warning, don't threaten and yell, but be firm.

Things to Try

1. At this level of discipline it is wise to talk through the consequences that will result if the improper behavior continues. Ask your child what he or she thinks the next consequences should be. The response may surprise you. However, children may suggest more severe consequences than are necessary, but you can temper this and help them become more realistic.
2. When other children are acting up, you might use that as an opportunity to pull your own child aside and talk through the situation with her. What does she think should happen or be the consequences for that behavior?
3. Have your child help you create some "warning signs" and place them around the house. For example: "Warning: ONLY LOVE SPOKEN HERE"; "Warning: WATCH FOR LOOSE TONGUE"; "Warning: LOVE ONE ANOTHER"; "Warning: SPEND MY TIME WISELY."

Being patient and kind are reflections of God's character, and this level of discipline requires these attributes even more than the other levels. A warning by its very nature is an attempt to help people see that what they are doing is wrong and to give them a chance to fix it. Many biblical characters needed a second chance (think of Abraham, Jacob, David, and others), and God graciously gave them opportunities to repent.

STUDY QUESTIONS

1. Think of times when you have been given a second chance. How did it make you feel? Why is it a good learning principle?

2. What are some things that your children really have a hard time remembering? What would be some good ways to help them remember so that you do not have to nag them about these things?

3. Do you remember a time when God gave you a second chance? If it is appropriate, share this with your children and tell them what you learned from it.

4. What warning signs would you like to put up around the house to help your children learn specific principles?

TIME TO PRACTICE

Think about the best way to handle the following situation:

You have told your six-year-old daughter to wash her hands before she sits down for dinner. This is the third time you have had to remind her to do this. Instead of yelling or getting angry, how can you help your daughter remember to do this from now on?

5

A Wise Parent Disciplines— Enforcing the Guidelines

If you don't like their rules, whose would you use?"
—CHARLIE BROWN, *PEANUTS*

only remember once being slapped my mother, but I will never forget it. I was about fourteen years old, and I had been very mouthy and had been sent to my room. Then my mother came in to talk with me about my behavior. I don't remember what she said, but I do remember that I told her to "shut up." Immediately I felt a stinging pain across my face. I had clearly overstepped the boundary, and I knew it. I also knew that my mother loved me, that she did not deserve to be treated like that, and that I deserved the slap. Even today when I think back on it, I am sorry that I treated my mother that way.

I doubt that most child psychologists today would recommend this type of punishment, and if it was a common occurrence I believe it would be wrong. But I deserved the punishment I received that day, and that slap taught me a valuable lesson. I never spoke that way to my mother again.

I had crossed a clearly established guideline, and my mother enforced the rule.

Encourage your children to respect proper authority. At home, in school, and in other areas of their lives, your children need to know the importance of respecting authority. It is a simple fact that some things cannot or will not be changed. Certain rules must be followed. Help your children understand that it is harmful to them, as well as to everyone else, to have constant arguments, fights, and problems with peers and adults. Let your child see how his or her misbehavior affects other people.

LEVEL 3: ENFORCING THE GUIDELINES

Principle 1: A Reprimand with Non-Corporal Punishment

A wise parent knows how and when to give a calm but firm reprimand and follow through with any consequence(s).

Your six-year-old just got her first two-wheel bike. You want her to wear a bike helmet. Sometimes she remembers, sometimes she doesn't. At first, you remind her to give her a chance to get used to remembering the helmet. If she doesn't show improvement, you give her a warning and talk about what consequence there will be if she doesn't wear her helmet the next time (it really doesn't matter at this point if she doesn't *remember* to wear it or if she is *choosing* not to wear it). If the next time she rides her bike she doesn't wear her helmet, it is time for you to reprimand her and to follow through with the consequence. We'll talk about how to reprimand appropriately and effectively. But first, let's look at what Proverbs has to say on the subject.

Proverbs uses the Hebrew word *yākaḥ* ("rebuke") to convey the idea of a reprimand. In Hebrew the word carries not only the meaning "to rebuke, to reprove, to correct, to convince or convict" but also implies exposure of one's sin and calls a person to repentance. Even though a reprimand is stern, Proverbs presents it as a positive method of discipline:

> Whom the LORD loves He reproves, even as a father corrects
> the son in whom he delights (3:12 NASB).

God himself uses rebuke or reprimand when necessary with His children, but it is clear from this proverb that He does it in love to correct us.[1]

To reprove someone means to express disapproval or admonish someone for inappropriate behavior. God does that for His children in a number of ways. Sometimes it may be through our conscience—we do something wrong and our conscience starts to bother us. Sometimes it may be through other people—we have done something that hurts someone and he or she brings it to our attention. Maybe it will be through prayer, God's Word, a sermon, or some circumstance, but somehow we determine that God is not pleased with something we have done.

As parents, we need to do the same thing with our children: to reprimand or reprove them, in love, so that they understand that their behavior is not acceptable and that they need to change. To do this wisely, we first need to take the time to find out what really happened—to be fair and just in judging a situation. Proverbs says:

> It is wrong to show favoritism when passing judgment. A judge
> who says to the wicked, "You are innocent," will be cursed by
> many people and denounced by the nations. But blessings are
> showered on those who convict the guilty (24:23–25).

---

1. For additional references, see: Proverbs 1:8-19, 20-31; 2:11-19; 3:27-35; 4:14-27; 5:7-23; 6:1-11, 32-35; 7:24-27; 8:32-36; 9:4-6; 10:5-10; 23:22-23.

What are the principles of these verses? Wrong behavior should not be tolerated; wrong behavior should be confronted for what it is. The person who carries through with this process will, in the long run, be a blessing. But not everyone will respond in the same way to a reprimand:

A single rebuke does more for a person of understanding than a hundred lashes on the back of a fool (17:10).

Some people are more teachable than others when it comes to changing behavior. And sometimes well-chosen words in the form of a reprimand are more effective than corporal punishment.

[A] survey of more than 1,500 parents in 27 states, Canada, and Puerto Rico gives a behind-closed-doors look at how parents discipline their kids. Methods ran the gamut from the matter-of-fact (removing privileges) to the chaotic (yelling) to the physical (spanking).

Parents said they most often used one or more of these strategies:

- Time-outs: 42%
- Removing privileges: 41%
- Sending to bedroom: 27%
- Yelling: 13%
- Spanking: 9%

The survey was given to parents of kids aged 2–11 years before the children's "well child" doctor visits.

One of the best examples of a reprimand is the Old Testament story about David and Bathsheba (2 Samuel 11). After King David had an adulterous affair with Bathsheba, he arranged to have her husband killed in battle in an attempt to cover up the sin. God then sent Nathan the prophet to rebuke David (2 Samuel 12). To do this, the wise Nathan tells David a story about a rich man with many sheep and cattle and a poor man with one small lamb that was like a family pet. The rich man callously takes the poor man's lamb and kills it for a meal for a visitor instead of using one of his own. David is furious when he hears this. He declares that the rich man deserves to die and must make four-fold restitution for the lamb. Nathan immediately confronts David and declares, "You are that man!" David realizes that he has just convicted himself and confesses his guilt.

God used the truth to convict David, and the reprimand struck home. When we remind our children of the truth about their behavior, it may hurt, but they know we are right. This will work especially well when you have already talked about the consequences of a certain action. Then when they misbehave, you remind them of the consequences that you have already discussed.

Let's Apply It

There is a right way and a wrong way to deliver a verbal reprimand to a child: **A reprimand should always criticize the behavior, not the child.**

We want to voice our disapproval of what the child did, not shame or demean the child. If you hear yourself saying words like "you always…" or "you never…," you are on the wrong track. Nobody "always" or "never" does something. If you start your reprimand with words like "You idiot, I told you not to do that," you are tearing down your child rather than focusing on the behavior that needs to change.

Some other classic statements to avoid—things people tend to say in anger—are: "You'll never amount to anything." "You're just like [your father, your mother, your sister, your brother]." "How many times have I told you not to do that? Won't you ever learn?"

KIMBERLEE SAYS:

I noticed a little boy at the school where I used to work. His name was Juan, and he was in second grade. Juan always had his head hanging down and looked so sad. I wondered about him, as his sadness touched my heart. Then I saw why Juan was so sad. One day after school I saw Juan and his mother leaving his classroom. Juan dropped some papers on the ground. As he stopped to pick them up, his mother yelled, "You are such a klutz! You're always dropping things. No wonder no one wants to play with you. You probably can't even catch a ball!" You can imagine how this made Juan feel.

Many times parents are not this direct with their critical statements to their children, but they can be just as devastating. Parents do need to be careful how they phrase things when they are reprimanding their children. Being criticized by someone we look up to and love can be devastating. Learning to teach without being critical takes time and practice.

Instead of attacking the child, we need to direct our disapproval toward the behavior itself. Instead of "You never remember to take out the garbage," a better reprimand would be, "This is the third time this week that you did not take out the garbage. I expect you take out the garbage (state how often) every day (specify a time) after dinner. If you don't take out the garbage tomorrow (here's what will happen), you will lose TV privileges tomorrow night (or whatever consequence you think is fitting)."

Keep the reprimand short. One sentence telling your child what he or she specifically did wrong is sufficient, especially if you say it immediately following the misbehavior. You can also tell your child how you feel at the moment. Pick *one* emotion (for example, disappointed, angry, upset, or frustrated). Allow a few moments of silence so that what you've just said can sink in. This will also help you resist the temptation to keep lecturing.

Sometimes the discipline process can stop there—no consequence other than a reprimand is needed. At other times we need to follow through with a consequence. When this is the case, be matter of fact in your follow-through: "Since you chose not to take out the garbage, you also chose not to have TV privileges tonight."

KIMBERLEE SAYS:

Marcia was a divorced mom with two boys, ages 6 and 9, and she was having a tough time getting them to mind her. We implemented a chart program where the boys would earn points each time they listened, followed directions, or did something kind without being asked. These points could never be taken away once they were earned, and they could be turned in each week toward prizes, or saved up for a night out with Mom. Both boys wanted to save up points for a night out with Mom. This was very eye-opening, causing Marcia to realize that she was not spending enough quality time with her boys. Implementing time with each of the boys every night (instead of having them earn time with Mom) strengthened their relationship and made earning points even more fun for the boys. When last I spoke with Marcia, she told me that the boys could "donate" some or all of their points to earn a trip to Sea World! They had to do this together, so they would learn about team work.

There are a variety of consequences parents can choose, such as time outs, withholding something the child likes (e.g., a favorite toy or activity), extra chore(s), or withholding an allowance. Whatever you choose, it's important to tell your children that you're confident they will make a better choice next time. A pat on the back with a smile can help reassure them you're still on their side even though you are upset with their behavior.

When it comes to consequences, there are both effective and ineffective ways to follow through on misbehavior: **Children learn best when the consequences are somehow related to the misbehavior.**

> You should also use logical consequences. For example, if your child doesn't stay in the car seat, then the car doesn't go. If he throws food on the floor, then he doesn't get any more and may be hungry (and if your child is old enough, have him help clean the floor).

Sometimes we can allow natural consequences to go along with our reprimand. When my wife, Cathy, was a girl, her parents bought her a doll to take on vacation to entertain her during the long hours of driving in the car. Eventually she got bored and decided to hold her doll by the leg outside the window (this was before the days of air conditioned cars and four-lane highways). Her parents warned her that if she continued to do that, she'd lose the doll in the wind and they wouldn't go back to get it. What happened? You guessed it. She persisted in holding the doll in the wind, the doll broke, and Cathy was left holding just a plastic leg. Of course she cried and begged to go back for the doll. But her parents followed through on what they had promised, and Cathy learned that she might not like the consequences if she chose to misbehave.

When I was young, my parents warned me repeatedly not to play softball in the vacant lot behind our house because there were houses so close to it. They were stern in their warning and pointed out that if I didn't quit I'd break a window and would have to pay for it. Then the fateful day came when I hit a wild foul ball and it broke a window. I can remember not wanting to tell my parents after all their warnings. But I did, and sure enough, they had me pay for the window.

As our kids get into their teens, some of their behaviors may become patterns or habits that can influence their spiritual life. When I was an adolescent, I had a problem with my temper and would sometimes get into fights. As a Christian, I always asked God to forgive me, but I still continued to fight. One day in high school I got into a fight with another boy after class. We fought in the hallway, then continued down some cement steps. I pushed him, and he turned and punched me in the face. I fell and hit my head on the steps. Six hours later I woke up in the hospital with a brain concussion. It took these sobering natural consequences for me to realize that it was time to learn to control my anger and quit fighting. I knew that God wasn't pleased with my actions and that I had been a bad example spiritually.

Not surprisingly, parents sometimes feel overwhelmed by the stress of bringing up teenagers. But there are steps we can take to make things better. We can begin by remembering our own adolescence. Asking ourselves questions like "How much did I share with my parents?" "How critical and argumentative was I at that stage?" and "What were my worries and dreams?" can help us accept our teens' behavior better.

Obviously there are times when allowing a natural consequence isn't safe. Going back to the bike helmet example, you could let your six-year-old daughter fall, and she'd learn that the natural consequence of not wearing a bike helmet is that you get hurt. But you obviously don't want her to suffer a head injury to learn the importance of wearing a helmet. Some other type of consequence, like putting the bike away for a day or two (or longer if the child is older), might help her understand that you are serious about enforcing this rule.

We also have to be careful to choose consequences we can actually follow through on. "If you throw sand again, we'll never come back to the park" is unreasonable. However, immediately leaving the park for the day is logical, reasonable, and directly relates to the misbehavior ("You don't get to continue to play with others if you throw sand at them").

Parents can easily waver when it comes to following through with consequences. So be calm, be firm, be reasonable, and be consistent. No arguments, no bargains.

KIMBERLEE SAYS:

I can't count how many single mothers I have met that start dating a man and allow him to handle the misbehavior of their children. Reprimands and discipline should never come from a new significant other. Doing this can cause a child to rebel and refuse to respect authority, or can create an overly passive child who is bullied by everyone.

Points to Remember

1. Reprimands will be necessary, for seldom do children learn something the first time. But don't expect perfection. Remember how gracious God is with His children.

2. Reprimand carefully. Each child receives this type of discipline differently.

3. Allow the consequences of the discipline time to have the desired effect. If you remember a time when you needed to be reprimanded, share that with your child if it is appropriate.

4. Criticize the behavior, not the child.

5. Make sure the consequences are somehow related to the misbehavior.

6. Assure your children that you still love them, even though you are disappointed or upset with them.

Priniciple 2: A Reprimand with Corporal Punishment

*A wise parent knows when to use non-abusive,
corporal punishment.*

Warning: Proceed with caution. Use this principle only when other levels have failed to produce positive results.

National Public Radio commentator Link Nicoll married and had children later in life. When it came to childrearing, she did her homework, reading many books by child-rearing experts. She now realizes that sometimes those experts have their limits.

Last week on our summer vacation, my husband and I did the unthinkable: We spanked our three-year-old son. We are baby boomers. We are not supposed to spank. That was something our parents did to us. No, we, the enlightened generation, are supposed to nurture our child's inner desires. We're supposed to allow him to get in touch with his true self.

It is at points like this that we all wonder, *What should I do.*

The problem is our son has been getting a little too wild. During our summer road trip, he discovered how to get out of his car seat. My husband and I have had many discussions about child discipline. We rely on today's child-rearing books and one thing is clear: Spanking is practically synonymous with child abuse. Instead, we practice the strategy of giving our child choices, letting him make his own mistakes so he can learn from the consequences. So on this car trip, with the issue of car safety, we said, "Dear, you have a choice between getting back in your car seat or sitting along the highway in a boiling car. Which would you prefer?"

We have all been there, haven't we!

After hours of this approach, lots of high-pitched whining and no success, my husband finally shouted, "If you don't get back in your car seat and stay there, I'm going to spank you!" There was silence. I couldn't believe he said the S-word. "You're going to have to follow through on that," I said, echoing another child-rearing tip I had read.

My son ignored my husband's demand. He jumped up, spun around and pressed his face against the back window and laughed. I looked at my husband; he looked back.

It is easy to see that this was clearly a teaching moment, since the child knew full well what he was supposed to do but merely chose not to do it.

We pulled over into a nearby Wendy's parking lot. My husband got out of the car and opened my son's door. He took him out of the back seat. I covered my eyes, but I could still hear. I counted: one, two, three, four. My husband got back into the car and said calmly, "I spanked him with his pants on."

"Good," I said, relieved.

We got back on the highway and for the first time in hours, our child was still. Two hours later, when we reached our destination, we realized that the rest of our trip had been unusually cheerful. The spanking had not hurt him, and it had not hurt us. The hard part was realizing that maybe, just maybe, a type of discipline once used by our parents had actually worked.

There has been much debate in recent years about spanking. Some believe it should be used judiciously; others believe it is never warranted, and that it is tantamount to child abuse. As we begin our discussion of this principle, therefore, we begin with a strong warning:

There is never any reason or justification for causing physical harm or danger to a child, even when spanking.

Among physicians, 59 percent of pediatricians and 70 percent of family physicians support the use of corporal punishment, although approval is greatest when it is used to correct dangerous behavior.

While the verses from Proverbs that we will look at in this section imply that there is a place for physical discipline, we believe that spanking should be used rarely, and then only one or two swats on the bottom with the hand. This should be done without anger, yelling, or losing control. Spanking is not advised for children under the age of eighteen months and rarely, if ever, over the age of ten. Other forms of discipline should be used outside of this age range. Remember:

The goal of spanking is not to induce pain, but to teach the child that his or her behavior has crossed a boundary line. It is used only when the child has not responded appropriately to lower levels of discipline.

KIMBERLEE SAYS:

I have many horrific stories from my days working at Child Protective Services. One of these was an 8-year-old girl who came to school with lacerations all over her back and the back of her legs. She explained to her teacher that she was whipped with a belt because she would not go to bed with the lights off. In talking to her mother about this, we learned that her boyfriend was sick of her and her daughter fighting about the lights, so he "took care of it." The boyfriend explained that he "lost it" and "went out of control."

In discussing the previous discipline levels, we chose verses that are representative of principles found in the book of Proverbs. But for this level, we will discuss each verse that applies to physical discipline, not only because some of them have been the focus of much debate, but also so that we can fully understand what Proverbs has to say about physical discipline. For example:

He who withholds his rod hates his son, but he who loves him disciplines him diligently (13:24 NASB; see also 22:15).

Some people find it difficult to reconcile a harsh-sounding verse like this from the Old Testament with New Testament teaching, like the Golden Rule of Matthew 7:12: "Do to others what you would have them do to you" (NIV).

On a spring day, Susan Lawrence was flipping through a magazine, *Home School Digest*, when she came across an advertisement that took her breath away. In it, "The Rod," a $5 flexible whipping stick, was described as the "'ideal tool for child training."

"Spoons are for cooking, belts are for holding up pants, hands are for loving, and rods are for chastening," read the advertisement... for the 22-inch nylon rod. It also cited a biblical passage, which instructs parents not to spare the "rod of correction."

The ad shocked Lawrence, a Lutheran who home-schools her children and opposes corporal punishment. She began a national campaign to stop what she sees as the misuse of the Bible as a justification for striking children. She also asked the federal government to deem The Rod hazardous to children, and ban the sale of all products designed for spanking. Lawrence says striking children violates the Golden Rule from the Gospel of Matthew in the New Testament: "In everything do to others as you would have them do to you."

So what does the word "rod" actually mean?

The Hebrew word for "rod" in Proverbs 13:24 is *shebeṭ* and means "rod, staff, club, scepter." It is used to describe instruments that were used to hit (Exodus 21:20; Isaiah 10:15; Proverbs 10:13; 22:15), beat out spices (Isaiah 28:27), and as a weapon (2 Samuel 23:21; 1 Chronicles 11:23). Thus, the Hebrew word can signify a range of meanings that include various types of instruments, from a "stick" to a "rod," depending on its purpose. It is also used *figuratively* to describe God's punishment of Israel (Isaiah 10:5, 24; 30:31; 14:29).

The Hebrew word for "diligently" in this verse is the verb *shaḥar* which means "to seek earnestly, early, diligently." In this verse the implication is that parents should discipline their children when necessary and without delay.

It was probably common in the ancient Near East to use a rod for discipline, but this does not mean that we must use the same instrument of discipline today—merely that we must use some form of discipline and use it consistently. Thus while some form of fair and consistent discipline is necessary, the use of a "rod" itself is not crucial.

Several proverbs also point out that the lack of parental discipline can lead to severe consequences.

Discipline your children while there is hope. If you don't, you will ruin their lives (19:18).

Sin in our life, left unchecked, can lead to more and greater sins. Just as a drug addict who has to take more and more drugs to get the same kind of high can easily be lured into a drug overdose without even realizing it, so sin can lure us into more and greater sins. Building on this principle, this proverb points out that your child's bad behavior, left unchecked, could in time escalate into behavior that will ruin his or her life and perhaps even, in time, lead to death—the ultimate punishment of separation from God.

Don't fail to correct your children. They won't die if you spank them. Physical discipline may well save them from death (23:13–14).

The Hebrew word for "correct" (*mûsar*) means "to discipline, chasten, admonish" and is sufficiently broad enough to cover a range of discipline techniques.

In these two verses the implication is that discipline can ward off a child's untimely death. The background for this statement can probably be traced to Deuteronomy 21:18–21 where a son who was habitually drunk, rebellious, and would not listen to his parents was to be taken to the elders of the city to be stoned (our discussion of society's role in discipline will be discussed in chapter 7).

The emphasis in Proverbs 19:18 and Proverbs 23:13–14, therefore, is on how important discipline is in helping to change or improve the child's character. We learn in Proverbs 22:15 that "A youngster's heart is filled with foolishness, but discipline will drive it away." Some of us might react to that statement by arguing that it's too strong—that overall we have "good kids." But the principle here addresses what kids tend to do when not checked by discipline—what will happen if they're allowed to act on their natural impulses and desires alone.

This was highlighted on our recent family vacation. My family and I decided to go to a little amusement park and ride the go-karts. And before we even started our ride, we saw the little menace. He was probably about nine years old, and when he came into the pit stop area, rather than applying the brakes, he ran right into the car in front of him. This apparently was his way of stopping, even though the cars clearly said "No bumping" on them.

I was glad this kid was in the race before us so at least we would be safe from his dangerous driving. But no sooner had I thought that than he was running through the line to get back onto the go-karts. *Oh no, he's going to be in my race,* I thought.

The first lap was fine—we didn't even see him. But then up ahead, swerving from side to side so that no one could pass him, was the little menace. As we got close to him, he did everything possible to keep us from passing. Then I got my chance to get around him and I took it. I was about halfway around when he turned his car right into the side of my car and tried to run me off the road. I guess he did not understand what "no bumping" meant. I got around him, and he ended up spun around on the track. What was interesting was that the minute he thought he might get into trouble, he pulled the innocent routine and made it look as if he had no idea how he got turned around on the track.

> In 2002 in the U.S. an estimated 896,000 children were determined to be victims of child abuse or neglect, 80 percent of which was committed by their parents. In that same year an estimated 1,400 children died from abuse or neglect.

On the next lap when he got close enough to see me again, he made an obscene gesture at me. Then he went around another lap or two really slow, obviously wanting us to catch up to him. He was out for vengeance. He tried again, and once again ended up sideways on the track, only this time he took a little girl with him.

For the rest of the time I managed to stay ahead of him, but I kept wondering, *Where are his parents?* And why did he get away with such bad behavior? My guess is that his parents had dropped him off to get some "peace and quiet." He had probably gotten away with the innocent look before, so he tried it again. But who is going to teach him how to behave?

People who have never been under authority will not easily somehow learn it. That is why the levels of discipline mentioned in Proverbs are crucial for us to use. It gradually teaches our children how to behave properly.

Both Proverbs 19:18 and Proverbs 23:13–14 address the reality that it is better to head off misbehavior and willfulness when the child is young than allow it to run wild and possibly lead in the adolescent years or later to run-ins with the law (more about this in chapter 7). In other words, severe misbehavior may merit severe disciplinary measure(s). The context suggests that it is better for a loving parent to go to this extreme than to allow children to continue on in self-destructive behavior that could lead to terrible consequences—even death.

This level of discipline should only be used when previous levels have not curbed a child's misbehavior, and it should not do irreparable harm—the implication being that spanking should never be used in an abusive way.

And remember:

Discipline misused can have an equally detrimental effect on children.

What happens when the rules are broken?

- Just because rules are broken does not mean there shouldn't be any rules. When rules are broken, there needs to be some consequence but this has to be carefully thought through.

- Whatever you decide, your teenager is likely to see it as punishment and be resentful, but if you don't take any action you are making it more difficult for yourself next time.

- Before you jump in and react, look for the cause. Listen first to what your teenager has to say.

- Make consequences that fit the rules that were broken, e.g., if they come home late, they have to come home earlier next time. Only make consequences that you can follow through with and, remember, don't make too many or they won't work.

- What works for one young person might not work for another.

- Your teenager must know very clearly beforehand what the consequences will be by talking over these sorts of things together. It is important that any consequences you set are not so heavy that they stop your teenager from wanting to try.

- Set consequences that can be quickly completed and then give your teenager a chance to try again, e.g,, "You came home very late after we agreed on a time, so tomorrow I will pick you up" or "Tomorrow you will have to stay home."

Parents whose discipline is overly harsh or restrictive will cause their children to have angry, resentful attitudes. Ephesians 6:4

says, "Don't make your children angry by the way you treat them. Rather, bring them up with the discipline and instruction approved by the Lord."

> The rod and reproof give wisdom,
>> But a child who gets his own way brings shame to his mother (29:15 NASB).

This verse implies that if a child does not have his or her will curbed, that child will become uncontrollable and bring shame to the family. While the word "rod" undoubtedly suggests some type of corporal punishment, as we pointed out above, it is possible that the word came to signify a broader range of disciplinary methods and not just physical discipline. The verse states that verbal instruction and physical discipline may be used together to foster wisdom. Even modern child psychologists have shown that this combination can be the most effective in curbing misbehavior (you will find more discussion on this in the next chapter, "The Spanking Dilemma").

Although this proverb refers only to the mother, this does not mean that the mother is solely responsible for discipline. After all, fathers can be equally embarrassed by the actions of their stubborn, rebellious children.

A strong contrast is also made here between letting a child "get his own way" and using "the rod and reproof." In this case, the phrase "rod and reproof" is referring to some form of discipline or correction and may suggest both physical and verbal forms, implying that physical discipline can be effective in curbing a child's will.

Here, as in many other areas, parents need to learn balance. On the one hand we want to let our children have freedoms and express themselves, especially as they grow older. On the other hand, we all have sinful natures that, if left unchecked, can lead us into destructive lifestyles.

> Says Cheri Weeks, a child psychologist and a mother of three in Los Angeles: "I know that my parents have always been supportive, and these were the same people who spanked me when I was growing up. My parents' motto and my motto is that I need to discipline my children so that the world doesn't have to."

Pastor Darryl DelHousaye uses a concise teaching statement that captures the principle of this verse: "Curb the will; nurture the child." Of course it takes time and energy to curb the will, especially with strong-willed children. But kids who haven't had their wills curbed, or haven't learned how to control their wills, may find it hard to stay within society's laws and expectations. Commentator Derek Kidner says, "To withhold discipline is neither a compliment nor a kindness; and the opportunity passes."

Let's Apply It

I remember my mother saying, "This is going to hurt me more than it does you." As a child, I doubted it; however, now that I am a father and have had to discipline my own sons, I understand exactly what my mother meant.

This level of discipline (A Reprimand with Non-Abusive Corporal Punishment) is reserved for times when the previous levels of discipline have not been successful and the destructive behavior still continues. When the child has been sufficiently warned and has been told clearly what the improper behavior is, it is time to follow through on the discipline. But remember:

The parent must never discipline in anger and must be consistent in following through with the stated discipline.

Wise parents know their children well enough to know the best forms of punishment for them and use spanking as the last resort.

As we pointed out earlier in this section, we believe that it is wise when spanking your child to use only your hand on the child's clothed bottom so that you know exactly how much pain you are inflicting. It is also wise to use only the amount of discipline necessary to curb the improper behavior, and is best to err on the side of caution.

I remember once when after spanking my son, he got off my knee and boldly announced, "That didn't even hurt." So he went right back on my knee and got two more swats. Afterward he said he was sorry and we hugged. I used only the amount of discipline that seemed necessary, but obviously the first time it wasn't quite enough.

The 'Dos' and 'Don'ts' of Parent-Teen Communication:

- Don't argue with the way your teen sees things. Instead, state your own case and speak from that. "I have a different opinion," "This is what I believe," and "This is the way I see it."

- Don't talk down to your teenager. There's nothing more irritating than a condescending tone.

- Don't lecture or preach. Again, this only provokes hostility. Besides, the average teenager goes "deaf" after hearing about five sentences.

- Don't set limits you can't enforce.

- Do focus on the behavior, not the person.

- Do think ahead to what you will say and how you will say it.

- Do keep your messages clear and concise.

- Do stick to one issue at a time.

I can remember receiving several spankings when I was a child. Each time I knew what I was being punished for, and afterward my mother (my parents were divorced) regularly hugged me. I knew my mother loved me, and in some sense it felt good to know where the boundaries were. I was never abused, but when a spanking was necessary I knew very clearly why it was being administered.

One of the most important parts of child-raising is to make sure that your children know you love them and that you keep the communication lines open with them. I have not had to spank my children often, but I can remember a time when one of them had been acting up all day and we had gone through each of the discipline levels and it was time for a spanking. I made sure that he knew what he was being punished for and then had him lay across my lap. I swatted him twice on the bottom and he began to cry. We hugged and he said he was sorry and it was over. His attitude was greatly improved and he knew exactly where his boundaries were.

Build the Relationship

- Work on your relationship with your son or daughter first, because no discipline will be successful unless this is the basis. Having a good relationship takes time.

- Often you need to do things together on their terms. Listen to their ideas without trying to force your ideas on them. Take an interest in what is important to them and you will have a good baseline to work from.

- Trusting your teenager is an important part of your relationship. Trust has to be earned by both of you. Remind yourself that your teenager is struggling with lots of new feelings and his behavior could be showing genuine unhappiness which needs your concern.

And remember: there is more than one kind of abuse. Studies have shown that verbal abuse is just as damaging, sometimes even worse, than physical abuse, and it can lead to physical abuse. So watch what you say.

Never say things that you do not plan to follow through on, and never say things that you do not mean.

Use your language carefully and never say things like "Quit it or I'm going to beat you;" "Just wait till I get my hands on you;" "If you don't stop I'm going to strangle you;" or "Do you want me to smack you?"

Your response to misbehavior should be immediate, rather than the stereotypic statement, "Just wait till your father gets home—he'll give you a good spanking."

Divide the responsibility between both parents, so that one parent isn't the heavy-handed "cop." And be in agreement about how to discipline and what the consequences will be.

If you are a single parent, you will have to do most of the discipline by yourself. However, you will also be providing a great deal of the love and security that your child needs. Remember, God can give you the grace and love that your child needs. He knows your circumstances and He dearly loves you, so don't be afraid to ask Him for help.

The Family Research Council, in their careful and well-researched analysis of spanking, suggests the following guidelines:

1. Differentiate between "abusive hitting and nonabusive spanking."
2. Verbal corrections, time outs, and logical consequences should be the disciplinary methods of choice.
3. Spanking should be reserved for instances where non-compliance persists, and only if non-physical disciplinary methods have failed. "For very compliant children, milder forms of correction will suffice and spanking may never be necessary."

4. The child should receive "at least as much encouragement and praise for good behavior as correction for problem behavior."

5. "To avoid public humiliation or embarrassment," spanking should always be done in private.

6. Spanking "is inappropriate before 15 months of age and is usually not necessary until after 18 months. It should be less necessary after 6 years, and rarely, if ever, used after 10 years of age."

7. If spanking does not appear to work, a parent should never increase the severity of hitting. Professional help should be sought, and/or other disciplinary techniques tried.

8. A single slap to the hand of a young child, and one or two spanks to the buttocks for older children are recommended amounts.

9. Hugging the child afterward is recommended.

But what if a child remains defiant even after a spanking? What should a parent do?

At that point, it may be wise to seek some type of counseling or therapy to see if there are hidden emotional problems that need to be dealt with. The biblical text does appear to mention further levels of discipline, but it never says that a parent should inflict those levels of discipline. We will look at these in the next chapter.

Points to Remember

1. Children need boundaries, Even though they will test them, children still want the boundaries to be there.

2. Spanking is not recommended for children under 18 months or over 10 years of age. Other forms of discipline should be used with those age groups.

3. Modern research has shown that a combination of verbal correction with, when needed, physical non-abusive correction seems to work best for correcting behavior.

STUDY QUESTIONS

1. There appear to be times when the biblical text suggests a spanking is necessary. What would be the purpose for spanking?

2. Both parents need to be in agreement concerning this level of discipline, so what are some guidelines that parents should use before spanking a child?

3. In the midst of disciplining your children it is sometimes difficult to think through the various levels of discipline, so take some time now to list the various levels and the reasonable consequences for each level of disobedience.

4. Examine the answer to the previous question and think through your own disciplining techniques in the last month. Are there ways to improve your disciplining techniques? Are there ways to help your children not fall into the same habits or problems that lead to discipline?

TIME TO PRACTICE

Think about the best way to handle the following situation:

Your six-year-old son has pinched his four-year-old sister for the fourth time today. You have firmly reprimanded him, given him a time out, and taken away his toys. Nothing seems to be working. You feel frustrated and angry at your son. What should you do?

—◦~ ♥ ~◦—

6

The Spanking Dilemma

If you refuse to discipline your children, it proves you don't love them; if you love your children, you will be prompt to discipline them. —PROVERBS 13:24

As we have shown, the book of Proverbs encourages multiple levels of discipline, starting with encouraging the child to behave properly all the way up to non-abusive corporal punishment. Yet there has been significant debate over the final level—that is, the issue of spanking.

Psychologist H. Stephen Glenn says: "Corporal punishment is the least effective method [of discipline]. Punishment reinforces a failure identity. It reinforces rebellion, resistance, revenge, and resentment. And what people who spank children will learn is that it teaches more about you than it does about them—that the whole goal is to crush the child. It's not dignified, and it's not respectful."

Harriet McMillan of McMasters University and six of her associates say that their research shows a correlation between spanking during childhood and higher levels of adult depression, psychiatric problems, and addictions.

On the other hand, a number of child psychologists espouse conclusions similar to what we have found in the book of Proverbs.

In 2004, Dr. Robert E. Larzelere, Associate Professor of Psychology at the University of Nebraska Medical Center, presented a paper at the Conference on Parenthood in America in Madison, Wisconsin, which stated:

> Optimal disciplinary responses begin with less severe tactics, such as reasoning, but proceed to firmer disciplinary tactics when the initial tactics achieve neither compliance nor an acceptable compromise. The firmer tactics can be nonphysical punishment initially, with non-abusive physical punishment reserved as a back-up for the nonphysical punishment. This is consistent with many studies showing that a combination of reasoning and punishment is more effective than either one alone and with new evidence that this sequence enhances the effectiveness of milder disciplinary tactics with preschoolers.

What Larzelere recommends is similar to the various levels outlined in the book of Proverbs, starting with reasoning (we called it encouraging proper behavior) and working through the various levels up to non-abusive physical punishment.

However, this goes against many child psychologists and pediatricians who have argued that corporal punishment (i.e., spanking) is: ineffective; may trigger criminal, anti-social, violent, aggressive behavior later in life; has been linked to many adult problems; results in lower IQ as compared with children whose parents used other methods of discipline and control; can lead to abuse; can unintentionally cause serious physical damage; trains a child to use violence; and creates fear in the child.

What is interesting is that research has not shown a direct connection between reasonable and appropriate discipline and any of the problems mentioned above.

For example, M. L. Gunnoe and C. L. Mariner, in their study of 1,112 children aged 4 to 11, found that "for most children, claims that spanking teaches aggression seem unfounded." And Dan Olweus, in his study of adolescent boys, discovered that "remarkably, childhood aggressiveness has been more closely linked to maternal permissiveness and negative criticism than to even abusive physical discipline."

Dr. Lazelere also points out some of the weaknesses of recent research by those who are against non-abusive corporal punishment:

> This strange situation is reflected in research questions and methods, which often assume the correctness of the author's implicit beliefs. For example, few studies investigate differences between effective and counterproductive use of a particular disciplinary tactic, whether reasoning or punishment. Instead, the preferred disciplinary tactic is assumed to be invariably effective and the other one invariably ineffective, regardless how either one is used.

What appears to happen in modern research is that the researchers believe that spanking is abusive behavior and thus they link all forms of abusive behavior together (e.g., sexual abuse, physical abuse, verbal abuse). This being the case, it is no wonder that their research shows that abuse (or they say, spanking) causes many serious problems.

On the other hand, Diana Baumrind, research psychologist at University of California-Berkeley's Institute of Human Development, said in an address to the 2004 annual meeting of the American Psychological Association in San Francisco:

> We found no evidence for unique detrimental effects of normative physical punishment... I am not an advocate of spanking, but a blanket injunction against its use is not warranted by the evidence. It is reliance on physical punishment, not whether or not it is used at all, that is associated with harm to the child.

Baumrind, in her work with Elizabeth Owens on parenting styles, reported the results of their study on corporal punishment, which studied children from 1968, when they were preschoolers, to 1980, when they were early adolescents. The data indicated that the children of authoritative parents—described as parents who were loving, firm, and communicated well with their child—generally showed more individual initiative and social responsibility.

Detective Robert R. Surgenor, Berea, Ohio, Police Department, says:

Since 1982 in my city, the incidents of Domestic Violence cases where children physically assault their parents have increased 700%. The national statistics show an overall increase of almost 400%.

I am responsible for compiling all information on those offenses. I conduct interviews with the parents and child, along with school officials and employers of the child. What I find startling is that of all those kids arrested in my city for hitting their parents, only 1.9% received any type of corporal punishment as they were being raised. Less than 2% of these aggressive, angry children were spanked! The non-spanking "experts" contend that spanking a child makes them angry and aggressive. The exact opposite is true!

Baumrind's conclusions also showed that:

Studies of verbal punishment yielded similar results, in that researchers found correlations just as high, and sometimes higher, for total verbal punishment and harm to the child, as for total physical punishment and harm… What really matters is the child-rearing context. When parents are loving and firm and communicate well with the child [a pattern Baumrind calls authoritative] the children are exceptionally competent and well-adjusted, whether or not their parents spanked them as preschoolers.

If spanking were as detrimental as some child psychologists argue, then you would think that children's behavior would be improving, since far fewer parents are spanking their children these days. But quite the opposite seems to be true. At least this is what Tina Blue believes. In her online article "American Kids Really *Have* Changed," she says:

> Lisa, a 19-year-old friend of mine who has always loved children, and who since age 12 has babysat regularly as her primary source of income, just gave up babysitting—permanently. Her reasons are the same as those that caused me to close my home daycare in 1999, after 18 years of operation.
>
> Partly we just didn't want to deal with the parents anymore. Sure, some of the parents were absolutely wonderful. But all too many were outrageously exploitative. They demand far more than is reasonable and pay far too little—if they bother to pay at all...
>
> Parents also spoil their children terribly, even as they neglect them. The same parents who can't be bothered to remind a toddler or preschooler to use the bathroom, or who park the kid in front of a TV so they won't have to deal with him, will give in to almost any demand that child makes—and usually for the same reason. It's easier to give the kid whatever he wants in order to shut him up for a while.
>
> I'm sure there's a certain amount of guilt involved, too. After spending 40-60 hours away from the child during the week, the parents might well be reluctant to set limits or enforce discipline. Besides, parents who seldom see their child are rather like substitute teachers, since the child has spent most of his waking hours in the company of the babysitter. And we all know how kids act up for substitute teachers.

The same kid that minds the babysitter quite well might still turn into a demanding, disobedient tyrant whenever he is at home or anywhere else in the company of his parents.

But more often, the parents' failure to socialize their children or discipline them in any way means that the kids are just not very pleasant to be around, even in the daycare.

During the last few years I did daycare, I felt terribly frustrated by the fact that the children who were coming into my care past infancy were almost completely unsocialized. They had no idea of how to behave, no respect for anyone else or anyone else's property, no impulse control, and no toleration for any limits at all on their speech or behavior.

This story opens up another question: Who should discipline your child? It is important for you to think through this issue.

If your child is in a daycare setting, do you want the person in charge disciplining your child, or more specifically "spanking" your child? When children are young, they often need constant or regular correction, so at the very least find out the guidelines that the daycare uses for correction and determine if you agree with them.

[T]he Swedish experiment to reduce child abuse by banning spanking seems to be failing. In 1980, one year after this ban was adopted, the rate of child beatings was twice that of the United States. According to a 1995 report from the government organization Statistics Sweden, police reports of child abuse by family members rose four-fold from 1984 to 1994, while reports of teen violence increased nearly six-fold.

When a child gets a little older, things become more complicated. For example, we have decided that we do not want a teacher or principal of a school disciplining our children. First of all, in the book of Proverbs it is made very clear that discipline is the role of a parent. Second, we believe that a teacher or principal has not developed a loving relationship with our children and thus has not earned the right to do certain forms of discipline. As you make your own parental decisions, it would be very wise to ask a school for their discipline policy and make sure that you agree with it before sending your children to that school.

If correction does not start at home, it will happen nowhere else. What we have learned from the biblical passages and from recent psychological studies is that the discipline of our children requires a comprehensive structure of multiple layers that should be framed in a loving, structured family relationship.

Things to Remember

1. The book of Proverbs and some child psychologists espouse a similar structure of discipline.
2. Things are not always as they appear and even researchers have an agenda. When non-abusive spanking is linked together with other forms of abuse, the evidence gets skewed, suggesting any type of spanking is dangerous.
3. Each level of discipline must be carried out in a loving, caring family relationship.

STUDY QUESTIONS

1. There is little doubt that spanking can be misused and thus can be harmful. What are some proper guidelines that parents should follow to make sure their discipline is not harmful?

2. Parents must talk with their children about all levels of discipline, but especially spanking. What are crucial steps regarding spanking that need to be talked about?

3. What are the proper guidelines for spanking a child?

4. At what point is spanking no longer a proper method of discipline for a child?

TIME TO PRACTICE

Think about the best way to handle the following situation:

> Your good friend shares with you that their six-year-old daughter is so rebellious that she finds herself spanking her "all the time" and yet it does not curb her behavior. She asks your advice about discipline and spanking. What do you tell her?

7

Beyond a Parent's Responsibility

He who does not punish evil commands it to be done.
—LEONARDO DA VINCI

The book of Proverbs covers the whole range of discipline, including extreme disciplinary situations. However, the Bible makes it quite clear that at a certain point in extreme cases a parent's job is done and the government or other human structures take over.

LEVEL 4: GOVERNMENT'S ROLE IN DISCIPLINE
Principle: Continued Disobedience
May Bring Severe Punishment

Wise parents begin laying the groundwork for understanding boundaries when their children are young, when it is much easier to curb a child's will. Then, as their children grow, these parents gradually allow them to establish some of their own guidelines and maintain them. Once their children are grown, parents hope that they have instilled a good set of values in their children, but the ultimate decision lies with each child. Anne Frank correctly said, "Parents can only give good advice or put them on the right paths, but the final forming of a person's character lies in their own hands."

There comes a point when children have to make their own decisions about their behavior and will be held responsible for their behavior. And the truth is that wise and good parents can have unruly children (consider the biblical example of the righteous King

Hezekiah, 2 Kings 18–20, who fathered the wicked Manasseh, 2 Kings 21).

Serious sin in the lives of our children can lead to the need for serious punishment. However, the book of Proverbs does not suggest that parents are responsible to carry out this level of discipline. Notice that none of the words suggesting family relationships (parents, father, mother, or child) are used in this next verse. Also notice that the purpose for this severe discipline is for the person's own good—to remove evil.

> Physical punishment cleanses away evil; such discipline purifies the heart (20:30).

The "physical punishment" here means, literally, "stripes of wounding," probably referring to "stripes" or "strokes" that result in welts, bruises, or lacerations (e.g., from the use of a whip). This verse suggests that severe corporal punishment is an effective method to curb willful rebellion—a punishment that scours away the evil.

Through the years, some have misused Proverbs 20:30 to advise parents that a spanking must be hard enough to bruise or wound a child. This is certainly not the intent of the book of Proverbs, and it never mentions parents administering this punishment. The purpose for proper discipline is always to try to protect and spare a person from the consequences and agonies of an inappropriate lifestyle or behavior—the consequences of sin. Remember:

Biblical discipline always has redemptive purposes.

Government's Role in Discipline

No parent should ever inflict harm upon a child. In ancient Israel, judges and kings, not parents, were given authority to deal with extreme behaviors. In our society, we have given government, not parents, power to punish certain destructive behaviors or wrongdoing.

The idea of government having the right to punish is supported in Scripture, as Romans 13:3–4 indicates:

> The authorities do not frighten people who are doing right, but they frighten those who do wrong. So do what they say, and you will get along well. The authorities are sent by God to help you. But if you are doing something wrong, of course you should be afraid, for you will be punished. The authorities are established by God for that very purpose, to punish those who do wrong.

Peter says something similar in 1 Peter 2:13–14:

> For the Lord's sake, accept all authority—the king as head of state, and the officials he has appointed. For the king has sent them to punish all who do wrong and to honor those who do right.

Standards and judgments have changed throughout the millennia, but that government is responsible for certain forms of disciplinary punishment seems to be a constant. All nations have some type of progressive punishment, and severe punishment may curb a person's bad behavior and in the end possibly save his life.

In chapter 5 we talked about the principle in Proverbs 19:18: "Discipline your son [child] while there is hope, and do not desire his death" (NASB).

The rationale and motivation for disciplining your children "while there is hope" is to discipline them when they will listen and it will do some good. This is why we have suggested disciplining your child with age-appropriate discipline very early. Wise parents instill those guidelines into their children's lives when they are young and teachable, for they know that if they do not, there may come a time when their children will no longer listen to them.

If that happens, further discipline may lie beyond the parent's control.

Things to Remember

1. This level of punishment is not a parent's responsibility.
2. Severe punishment may deter some people from further destructive behavior that might harm themselves or others.
3. Biblical discipline always has redemptive purposes.

STUDY QUESTIONS

1. Why would God allow the government to take over certain forms of punishment?

2. Biblical discipline always has redemptive purposes, so what is the purpose for even severe forms of punishment?

3. Explain the rationale for the guidelines in Deuteronomy 21:18–21? Why would God command such severe forms of punishment?

4. Can you think of a time or place in the Bible when God uses some severe form of punishment? Can God still be a loving God and demonstrate this type of action? Why or why not?

TIME TO PRACTICE

Think about the best way to handle the following situation:

The son of one of your best friends has just been sent to prison for robbing a bank. Your friend comes to you and asks what he or she has done wrong. How would you respond to your friend, and how could you show a nice balance of both grace and truth in this situation?

8

God's Use of Discipline

My child, don't ignore it when the LORD disciplines you, and don't be discouraged when he corrects you. For the LORD corrects those he loves, just as a father corrects a child in whom he delights. —PROVERBS 3:11–12

Scripture tells us that God is the perfect Father and that He sometimes disciplines His children, even as adults (Proverbs 3:11–12; Hebrews 12:5–11). It would, therefore, be consistent for God to discipline us according to the wise guidelines and levels of discipline He has laid out for us in the book of Proverbs. In fact, the Bible demonstrates that God as the master parent regularly uses these various levels of discipline when dealing with His children. Let's consider, for example, God the Father's discipline in the life of the patriarch Abraham.

Abraham

Abraham starts out as a pagan, but gradually learns what God expects of him. The process is somewhat slow as God patiently works in Abraham's life using the various levels of discipline to guide and direct him; and in time Abraham learns what God expects of him and what he is to expect from God.

LEVEL 1: TEACHING THE GUIDELINES
Principle 1: Teach Appropriate Behavior

God begins by teaching Abraham the importance of obedience when He gives him the following promise:

> Then the LORD told Abram, "Leave your country, your relatives, and your father's house, and go to the land that I will show you. I will cause you to become the father of a great nation. I will bless you and make you famous, and I will make you a blessing to others. I will bless those who bless you and curse those who curse you. All the families of the earth will be blessed through you" (Genesis 12:1–3).

What an amazing encouragement to obey God. He promises progeny, blessings, a great reputation, protection, and blessing to all the families of the earth through Abraham, if only Abraham is willing to obey. Modern parents would do well to follow God's example here and instill a vision of the blessings their children will enjoy if they live within the confines of obedience. And just like Abraham, the children need to understand that if they fail to obey, then at least some of the blessings that they could have enjoyed may be forfeited.

Abraham realizes quite quickly that God's promise hinges on obedience and he heads toward Canaan. Like a wise parent God continues to remind Abraham of the promise and the blessings that he will enjoy if he continues to obey (Genesis 13:14–17; 15:12–21; 17:1–8).

Genesis 13:14–17 provides an interesting example where God reiterates the promise right after Abraham completely obeys God's command by separating from Lot. By so doing, God highlights the importance of total obedience.

Principle 2: Inform of Improper Behavior

Abraham is often informed of his improper behavior by other people (e.g., Pharaoh, Genesis 12:17–20; Sarah, Genesis 16:5–6;

Abimelech, Genesis 20:9–11), but God also reinforces to Abraham what would be improper behavior. In Genesis 17:14, God states, "Anyone who refuses to be circumcised will be cut off from the covenant family for violating the covenant." Here, God clearly states what actions or inactions would sever the covenant relationship.

God models good parenting skills by reinforcing that guidelines must be clear and that His children need to know exactly what is expected from them.

Principle 3: Explain the Negative Consequences of Sin

Genesis 17:14 clearly spells out the consequences for disobedience: Israel will be removed from the covenant blessings. The wise parent realizes that stating consistent consequences is a strong motivation for proper behavior.

LEVEL 2: REITERATING THE GUIDELINES
Principle: Give Appropriate Warnings

Even Abraham didn't always get it right and needed gentle exhorting. In Genesis 17:18, Abraham offers God an easier way, namely to use Ishmael as the promised seed, as if God needs an easier way to accomplish something. But God doesn't consent to it. He is still fairly gentle with Abraham, but He makes it clear that He will accomplish His purposes in His own way. (Imagine, for a moment, if God had settled for Abraham's suggestion. Abraham never would have known the joy of having a child through Sarah; but even worse, he would never have known the power of his God.)

Sometimes God likes to surprise His children, and sometimes we may set our sights far too low. Also, as a wise parent, God sometimes has to curtail a child's present joy so that he or she will be able to experience an even greater future joy.

LEVEL 3: ENFORCING THE GUIDELINES

Principle 1: A Reprimand and Non-Corporal Punishment

One of the clearest examples of a reprimand for Abraham comes from the mouth of the pharaoh of Egypt when he states, "'What is this you have done to me?' he demanded. 'Why didn't you tell me she was your wife?... Here is your wife! Take her and be gone!'" (Genesis 12:18–19).

Sarah also is reprimanded by the Angel of the Lord when she laughs at the prospect of having a child in her old age. The Angel of the LORD reminds her, "Is anything too hard for the LORD?" (Genesis 18:14).

Abimelech reprimands Abraham when he says, "'What is this you have done to us?' he demanded. 'What have I done to you that deserves treatment like this, making me and my kingdom guilty of this great sin? This kind of thing should not to be done! Why have you done this to us?'" (Genesis 20:9–10).

Notice that God allows natural consequences to discipline His children. It would have served little purpose for God to continue chastening Abraham when Pharaoh and the king of Gerar had already done a thorough job. God's response (or lack thereof) should be a lesson to us when we are reprimanding our children: sometimes they have had enough reprimand and now need our love and silence.

The Purpose of Godly Discipline

God uses these various levels of discipline with His children to refine us and perfect us, just as a refiner works with precious metals.

Tim Harrison gave the following example in a sermon at Crescent City Foursquare Church in February 2002:

> The story is told of a group of women that met for Bible study. While studying in the book of Malachi, chapter three,

they came across verse three which says: "He will sit as a refiner and purifier of silver."

This verse puzzled the women and they wondered how this statement applied to the character and nature of God. One of the women offered to find out more about the process of refining silver and to get back to the group at their next Bible study.

The following week, the woman called up a silversmith and made an appointment to watch him work. She didn't mention anything about the reason for her interest, beyond her curiosity about the process of refining silver. As she watched the silversmith work, he held a piece of silver over the fire and let it heat up. He explained that in refining silver, one needed to hold the silver in the middle of the fire, where the flames were the hottest as to burn away all the impurities.

The woman thought about God holding us in such a hot spot; then she thought again about the verse, "He sits as a refiner and purifier of silver." She asked the silversmith if it was true that he had to sit there in front of the fire the entire time the silver was being refined. The man answered yes, that not only did he have to sit there holding the silver, but he had to keep his eyes on it the entire time it was in the fire.

If the silver was left even a moment too long in the flames, it would be destroyed. The woman was silent for a moment.

Then she asked the silversmith, "But how do you know when the silver is fully refined?"

He smiled at her and answered, "Oh, that's easy—when I see my image in it."

Things to Remember

1. God, our Father, disciplines us because He loves us.
2. God knows exactly the best way to discipline us for our good.
3. Discipline refines and perfects us.

STUDY QUESTIONS

1. Why does God discipline His children? What would happen if He didn't?
2. Can you think of a time when you where disciplined by God? Can you tell your children about this?
3. How do you know when you are being disciplined by God?
4. Can you think of other biblical examples of God's discipline?

TIME TO PRACTICE

Think about the best way to handle the following situations:

Your daughter just turned five and is starting kindergarten for the first time. She returns home after the first day of school with a note from the teacher stating that she was reprimanded for grabbing another child's toy. How do you handle this with your child?

Your son is sixteen years old and got his driver's license last month. Today is the second time he returned the car with the gas gauge on empty. The first time he did this you gently but firmly told him that was not acceptable. What do you do this time?

9

❧ ♥ ❧

Praying for Our Children

God has given parents one of the most important jobs in the world—to raise our children to love and revere and serve the Lord. Someone has said that children are like wet cement. Whatever falls on them makes an impression. You have the awesome job of forming and making impressions on these children that God has given to you.

In the nineteenth century, the Scottish preacher Horatius Bonar asked 253 of his Christian friends at what ages they were converted. Here's what he discovered:

Under 20 years of age	138
Between 20 and 30	85
Between 30 and 40	22
Between 40 and 50	4
Between 50 and 60	3
Between 60 and 70	1
Over 70	0

Parents are given children at the most important time of their life: when they require someone to constantly care for their every need. We will train and care for those children until they are able to do things for themselves. In their path toward adulthood, they will need to be disciplined and corrected regularly along their way, and the wise guidelines found in the book of Proverbs provide the foundation for this discipline. These guidelines have been tried and found to be true throughout the generations and will certainly work for you if you follow them tenaciously.

FIVE PRINCIPLES TO REMEMBER

The book of Proverbs teaches the following principles about discipline, some explicitly and some implicitly:

1. **All children need some form of discipline.** Proverbs 22:15 states: "A youngster's heart is filled with foolishness, but discipline will drive it away." This general principle suggests that all children need some form of discipline (though not all children may need corporal punishment). But remember, each child is different and the same guidelines will not work on all children. Modify the guidelines to fit your specific situation.

2. **Use the least amount of punishment necessary to curb improper behavior.** The word "discipline" covers a wide range of disciplinary techniques, from instruction to spanking. Wise parents use a variety of levels of discipline when encountering improper behavior and use them in increasing severity until the behavior is curbed. Both reasoning and disciplinary techniques can be used to encourage proper behavior from a child. Wise parents start early with age-appropriate disciplinary techniques and are consistent and diligent in their follow-through. This is to be done early in a child's life, preferably in a neutral context before the improper behavior is demonstrated. Wise parents are also cognizant of the need to demonstrate proper behavior in their own everyday lives. This is one of the strongest means of conveying their message.

3. **Always discipline in love, never in anger, with the goal of helping the child.** Even God disciplines those whom He loves (Proverbs 3:12).

4. **Some forms of punishment are outside a parent's responsibility.** Wise parents realize that they are not allowed to administer certain forms of discipline; instead, they leave these forms to the appropriate branch of society.

5. **Draw on God for help.** One of my favorite verses is James 1:5: "If you need wisdom—if you want to know what God wants you to do—ask him, and he will gladly tell you. He will not resent your asking." Even the book of Proverbs reminds us that God hears the prayer of the righteous (Proverbs 15:29).

We as parents have the awesome responsibility of training our children to become godly, humble, mature, and wise adults. There are times when we wonder if this job is more than we can handle, and it is at those times that we need to call out to God for help and wisdom as Amy Carmichael expressed so beautifully in the following poem:

Father, hear us, we are praying,
Hear the words our hearts are saying;
We are praying for our children.

Keep them from the powers of evil,
From the secret, hidden peril;
Father, hear us for our children.

From the whirlpool that would suck them,
From the treacherous quicksand, pluck them;
Father, hear us for our children.

From the worldling's hollow gladness,
From the sting of faithless sadness,
Father, Father, keep our children.

Through life's troubled waters steer them;
Through life's bitter battles cheer them;
Father, Father, be Thou near them.

Read the language of our longing,
Read the wordless pleadings thronging,
Holy Father, for our children.

And wherever they may abide,
Lead them Home at eventide.

There comes a time when a parent's job is finished. We can still give advice when our children ask for it, but we have to take our hands off and let them make their own decisions (and mistakes). We pray that we have given them the essentials necessary for godly living, and we continue to pray for them daily, that they will have wisdom and maturity.

Until that day comes, let's use the years we have with our children to "teach [them] to choose the right path" to the best of our ability and with God's help, and pray that "when they are older, they will remain upon it" (Proverbs 22:6).

PRINCIPLES OF DISCIPLINE	EXAMPLES OF APPROPRIATE DISCIPLINE
Level 1: Teaching the Guidelines (Invest much time here) Children need to learn guidelines, even though they do not always understand why these guidelines are important. If they are important to you, then in time they will be important to them. Make sure they understand what is appropriate behavior in as many situations as you can.	
Principle 1: Teach Appropriate Behavior	1. Take advantage of every "teaching moment" possible. 2. Spend time with your children. They can learn many things just by watching you.
Principle 2: Inform of Improper Behavior	1. Talk about inappropriate behavior. 2. Talk about how to correct inappropriate behavior and what the correct action is in specific situations.
Principle 3: Explain the Negative Consequences of Disobedience	1. Talk through the appropriate consequences for certain types of behavior. 2. Discuss why there are sometimes negative consequences. 3. What are natural consequences for certain behaviors?
Level 2: Reiterating the Guidelines (Once again—intentionally make the guidelines clear and understandable) This step is not just putting off the inevitable. It is extremely important! Children will test boundaries to make sure they are important. Make sure the guidelines are understandable and that the child is well aware that a consequence is coming. The consequence must be justified and appropriate.	
Principle: Give Appropriate Warnings	1. Sometimes a clear warning about inappropriate action is all that is necessary. 2. Give the warning with an explanation of why something is incorrect behavior (same way as above, but explain why). 3. Reaffirm the importance of obedience and consequences.

Gentle

Increasing Severity

Level 3: Enforcing the Guidelines

Center on positive consequences. Use negative consequences when the former are not working. Be consistent and fair. Do not raise your voice. You do not have to be angry to enforce guidelines—in fact, you should not enforce them in anger. Think through them so that you know what your objective is with your child and where you are in the disciplining process. Make sure your children know you love them, but you are serious about their obeying.

Principle 1: A Reprimand and Non-Corporal Punishment	Possible Consequences: **START with Positive Consequences** Praise them for proper behavior Praise someone else for good behavior (proximal praise) Add some type of reward (but be careful not to get caught in a rut of always having to give a reward for every good behavior) Let them earn a surprise by obedience If they play nicely they will get to play longer If good, take them for a walk If good, earn a star on a chart If good, add a privilege Set goals for multiple appropriate actions **Negative Consequences** Hold the child's hand and say "No!" Put a toy away Remove the child from the situation Time out (increase time if needed) Limit time on enjoyable activity Remove a privilege Add a chore Curfew Grounding
Principle 2: A Reprimand and Non-Abusive Corporal Punishment	If above forms of discipline fail to correct the behavior, use this. Only use this discipline step on child from about 18 months to about 10 years old. If this fails to curb behavior, seek professional help.

Increasing Severity

BEYOND A PARENT'S RESPONSIBILITY	
Level 4: Government's Role in Discipline WARNING!	
Principle: Continued Disobedience May Bring Severe Punishment	Proverbs 10:31; 20:30

Notes

14   *Children are getting less moral* Virginia Education Association (http://www.veaweteach.org/resources_parents_detail.asp?ContentID =407).

15   *Rev. Arthur Allen* Dahleen Glanton, "Discipline or Abuse? Church Renews Spanking Debate," *Houston Chronicle* (1 April 2001).

15   *same pastor had been jailed* David Firestone, "Child Abuse at a Church Creates a Stir in Atlanta," *The New York Times* (30 March 2001).

16   *More than 2.5 million cases* American Academy of Pediatrics, "Child Abuse," n.p. (21 February 2008). Online: http://www.aap.org/publiced/BK0_ChildAbuse.htm.

17   *Bug us a little* This code was drawn up at the request of Rev. C. Galea and is reprinted from the *Pennsylvania School Journal*, published by the Pennsylvania State Education Association.

19   *During initial construction* Sermon Illustration, "Security," n.p. (23 January 2008). Online: http://www.higherpraise.com/illustrations/security_eternal.htm.

26   *The hope of every parent* National Education Association, "Discipline that Works," n.p. (18 July 2006). Online: http://www.nea.org/parents/tools/disc.html.

30   *Discipline properly involves* J. Burton Banks, "Childhood Discipline: Challenges for Clinicians and Parents," *American Family Physician* 66 (2002): 1447-52, 1463-4.

30   *In 1502, a large block* Modified from Jeffery Poms, "Was That Out-Loud?" Sermon on April 2002, n.p. [cited 25 May 2006]. Online: http://www.sermoncentral.com/ illustration_topic_results.asp?TopicName=Family& categoryname =Stories&topic_id=103.

31 *Statistics indicate* Virginia Youth Violence Project, School of Education, University of Virginia, "Parental Statistics," n.p. (17 July 2006). Online: http://youthviolence.edschool.virginia.edu/prevention/parent-statistics.html.

33 *The American Association of Pediatrics* "Nation's Pediatricians Issue Policy on Parental Discipline of Children," (6 April 1998). Online: http://www.nospank.net/n-b27.htm.

38 *If I like it* "Sermon Illustrations," n.p. (23 June 2006). Online: http://www.sermonillustrations.com/a-z/c/children.htm.

39 *Discipline should be* J. Burton Banks, "Childhood Discipline: Challenges for Clinicians and Parents," *American Family Physician* 66 (2002): 1447-52, 1463-4.

42 *[The] psychologists spent* Alan Loy McGinnis, *The Friendship Factor* (Minneapolis: Augsburg Publishing House, 1979), pp. 93–94.

44 *Positive reinforcement* J. Burton Banks, "Childhood Discipline: Challenges for Clinicians and Parents," *American Family Physician* 66, (2002): 1447-52, 1463-4.

48 *John Rosemead* "Living with Children," *The Charlotte Observer*, (19 July 2006).

50 *Setting limits* Elaine M. Gibson, "Setting Limits Is Easy…Enforcing Them Is Not," n.p. (18 July 2006). Online: http://www.healthyplace.com/Communities/Parenting/elaine/guidelines.html.

51 *Explain the rules* Gibson, Ibid.

56 *Initially a child* Dr. Sears, "8 Ways to Raise a Moral Child," n.p. (19 July 2006). Online: http://www.askdrsears.com/html/6/T120100.asp#T120200.

57 *In 1982* Ron Hutchcraft, *Wake Up Calls* (Chicago: Moody, 1990), p. 60.

57 *First, the Eskimo,* Paul Harvey's radio commentary quoted by Chris T. Zwingelberg (24 October 2005). Online: http://www.sermonillustrations.com/a-z/sin_slavery_to.htm.

59 *Adhesive tape* Dr. Richard Dobbins, *Homemade*, November 1987, "Sermon Illustrations," (27 May 2006). Online: http://www.sermonillustrations.com/a-z/s/sex_premarital.htm.

Notes

60 *Even more schools* Valerie Strauss, "For More Schools, Teaching Morals Is Right," *Washington Post*, 1 June 2004, p. A12.

67 *I once dealt* James Dobson, *New Dare to Discipline* (Wheaton, Ill.: Tyndale, 1992), pp. 27–28.

68 *All children misbehave* Robin F. Goodman and Anita Gurian, "About Discipline—Helping Children Develop Self-Control," NYU Study Center, n.p. (20 July 2006). Online: http://www.aboutourkids.org/aboutour/articles/discipline.html.

70 *Child misbehavior* Ibtisam S. Barakat and Janet A. Clark, "Positive Discipline and Child Guidance," University of Missouri, n.p. (20 July 2006). Online: http://muextension.missouri.edu/xplor/hesguide/humanrel/gh6119.htm.

72 *When adults make rules* Family Communications, "FamilyCares: Rules," n.p. (20 July 2006).

75 *Some rules are non-negotiable* Public Health Agency of Canada, "The Parent-Teen Relationship: How Parents Can Make the Most of It?" n.p. (20 July 2006). Online: http://www.phac-aspc.gc.ca/ncfv-cnivf/familyviolence/html/nfntsrelparentado-ado2_e.html.

82 *Encourage your children* "Discipline that Works," National Education Association, n.p. (23 July 2006). Online: http://www.nea.org/parents/tools/disc.html.

84 *[A] survey of more* Miranda Hitti, "Disciplining Kids: What Parents Try and Why," Connecticut PTA, n.p. (22 July 2006). Online: http://www.ctpta.org/parenting/discipline.htm.

88 *use logical consequences* Pediatric Advisor, "Toddler Discipline," University of Michigan Health System (22 July 2006). Online: http://www.med.umich.edu/1libr/pa/pa_toddisc_hhg.htm.

89 *parents sometimes feel overwhelmed* "The Parent-Teen Relationship: How Parents Can Make the Most of It?" Public Health Agency of Canada, n.p. Ibid.

91 *Last week on our summer vacation All Things Considered*, "Commentary: Surprising Benefits of Spanking" (24 August 2004), © 2004 National Public Radio. All rights reserved.

93 *Among physicians* F. K. McCormick, "Attitudes of primary care physicians toward corporal punishment." *Journal of the American Medical Association* 267 (1992): 3161–5.

94 *On a spring day* Patricia Wen, Globe Staff, "Sale of Spanking Tool Points Up Larger Issue," *The Boston Globe*, January 10, 2005. n.p. [cited 2 November 2005]. Online: http://www.boston.com/news/local/articles/2005/01/10/campaigner_targets_spanking_tools_sale/.

97 *In 2002* National Clearinghouse on Child Abuse and Neglect Information. Online: http://nccanch.act.hhs.gov.pubs/factsheets/canstats.cfm.

99 *What happens when the rules are broken?* Children, Youth and Women's Health Service, "Discipline (Teens)," Government of South Australia, n.p. (22 July 2006). Online: http://www.cyh.com/HeathTopics/HealthTopicDetails.aspx?p=114&np=122&id=1670#2.

101 *Says Cheri Weeks* Pamela Paul, "Is Spanking OK? *Time,* Time Bonus Section (May 2006).

102 *The 'Dos' and "Don'ts'* "The Parent-Teen Relationship: How Parents Can Make the Most of It?" Public Health Agency of Canada, n.p. (22 July 2006). Ibid.

103 *Build the Relationship* Children, Youth and Women's Health Service, "Discipline (Teens)," Government of South Australia, n.p. (22 July 2006). Ibid.

104 *Family Research Council* S. DuBose Ravenel and Den A. Trumbull, "Spare the Rod? New Research Challenges Spanking Critics," Family Policy Publication, The Family Research Council (October 1996).

108 *Optimal disciplinary responses* Http://parenthood.library.wisc.edu/larzelere.larzelere.html (as of July 15, 2004).

108 *M. L. Gunnoe and C. L. Mariner* PubMed, "Toward a developmental-contextual model of the effects of parental spanking on children's aggression." (17 July 2007). n.p. Online: http://www.nebi.nem.nih.gov/entrez/query.

108 *Dan Olweus* Dan Olweus, "Familial and Temperamental Determinants of Aggressive Behavior in Adolescent Boys: A Causal Analysis," *Developmental Psychology* 16 (1980):644–660.

109 *This strange situation* Robert E. Larzelere, "Combining Love and Limits," p. 82. See also: Larzelere, "A review of the outcomes of parental use of nonabusive or customary physical punishment," *Pediatrics* 98 (1996): 824–831.

109 *We found no evidence* Patricia McBroom, "UC Berkeley study finds no lasting harm among adolescents from moderate spanking earlier in childhood," n.p. (24 August 2001). Online: http://www.berkeley.edu/news/media/releases/2001/08/24_spank.html.

110 *Detective Robert R. Surgenor* "Christian Police Officer Speaks Out on Corporal Punishment," Christian Parent.net, n.p. (17 July 2006).

110 *Studies of verbal punishment* Diana Baumrind, "Child Care Practices Anteceding Three Patterns of Preschool Behavior," Genetic Psychology Monographs 75 (1967): 43-88.

111 *Lisa, a 19-year-old friend* Tina Blue, "American Kids Really *Have* Changed," August 11, 2003. n.p. [Cited 11 July 2006]. Online: http://www.childrensneeds.homestead.com/rudekids.html.

112 *[T] Swedish experiment* Den A. Trumbull and S. DuBose Ravenel, "Spare the Rod? New Research Challenges Spanking Critics," n.p. [Cited 18 July 2006]. Online: http: //people.biola.edu/faculty/Paulp/spare_the_rod.htm.

122 *The story is told* Tim Harrison in a sermon at Crescent City Foursquare Church in February 2002 entitled "Part 1: The Quest for Authentic Transformation," n.p. [Cited 11 November 2006]. Online: http://www.sermoncentral.com.

For Further Reading

Chapman, Gary. *The Five Love Languages for Teenagers*. Chicago: Northfield Publishing, 2000.

Chapman, Gary and Ross Campbell. *The Five Love Languages for Children*. Chicago: Northfield Publishing, 1997.

Kimmel, Tim. *Grace Based Parenting*. Nashville: Thomas Nelson, 2005.

Kimmel, Tim. *Raising Kids for TRUE Greatness*. Nashville: W Publishing Group, 2006.

Wegner, Paul D., "Discipline in the Book of Proverbs: 'To Spank or not to Spank'," *Journal of the Evangelical Theological Society* 48.4 (December 2005): 715–732.

Note to the Reader

The publisher invites you to share your response to the message of this book by writing Discovery House Publishers, P.O. Box 3566, Grand Rapids, MI 49501, U.S.A. For information about other Discovery House books, music, videos, or DVDs, contact us at the same address or call 1-800-653-8333. Find us on the Internet at http://www.dhp.org/ or send e-mail to books@dhp.org.